For Richard

WHAT WILL YOU DO WITH MY STORY?

Elizabeth Meakins

On behalf of the United Kingdom Council
for Psychotherapy

KARNAC

A line from the unpublished diaries of the late artist Partou Zia reproduced with the kind permission of Richard Cook.

The publishers wish to thank *The Independent* for agreeing to the reproduction of Elizabeth Meakins columns, Tales from the Therapist's Couch.

"The Jailer" taken from Collected Poems © Estate of Sylvia Plath and reprinted by permission of Faber and Faber Ltd. and Harper Collins, New York.

First published in 2012 by
Karnac Books Ltd
118 Finchley Road
London NW3 5HT

British Library Cataloguing in Publication Data

A C.I.P. for this book is available from the British Library

ISBN-13: 978-1-85575-792-9

Typeset by V Publishing Solutions Pvt Ltd., Chennai, India

Printed in Great Britain

www.karnacbooks.com

WHAT WILL YOU DO WITH MY STORY?

Other titles in the UKCP Series:

What is Psychotherapeutic Research? by Del Loewenthal

Diversity, Discipline and Devotion in Psychoanalytic Psychotherapy: Clinical and Training Perspectives by Gertrud Mander

Shakespeare on the Couch by Michael Jacobs

Dialogue and Desire: Mikhail Bakhtin and the Linguistic Turn in Psychotherapy by Rachel Pollard

Our Desire of Unrest: Thinking About Therapy by Michael Jacobs

Not Just Talking: Conversational Analysis, Harvey Sacks' Gift to Therapy by Jean Pain

The Muse as Therapist: A New Paradigm for Psychotherapy by Heward Wilkinson

The Emergent Self: An Existential–Gestalt Approach by Peter Philippson

Psychosis in the Family: The Journey of a Psychotherapist and Mother by Janet C. Love

Hidden Twins: What Adult Opposite Sex Twins Have To Teach Us by Olivia Lousada

Child-Centred Attachment Therapy: The CcAT Programme by Alexandra Maeja Raicar

The Three-Point Therapist by Hilary A. Davies

The Use of Psychoanalytic Concepts in Therapy with Families: For All Professionals Working with Families by Hilary Davies

Love: Bondage or Liberation: A Psychological Exploration of the Meaning, Values, and Dangers of Falling in Love by Deirdre Johnson

The Role of Brief Therapies in Attachment Disorders by Lisa Wake

Therapy with Children: An Existentialist Perspective by Chris Scalzo

Why Therapists Choose to Become Therapists: A Practice-Based Enquiry by Sofie Bager-Charleson

Attachment and New Beginnings: Reflections on Psychoanalytic Therapy by Jonathan Pedder

Addictive Personalities and Why People Take Drugs: The Spike and the Moon by Gary Winship

Why Can't I Help this Child to Learn? Understanding Emotional Barriers to Learning by Helen High

Psychotherapy and Spiritual Direction: Two Languages, One Voice? by Lynette Harborne

How Money Talks by Lesley Murdin

CONTENTS

ACKNOWLEDGEMENTS

There are a lot of people without whom this book could never have happened. Mostly they are those who have shared their stories with me, and I hope the benefits to them were equal to mine. I am fortunate to have work that I find immensely rewarding.

There were several people who read and commented on the manuscript for me. Noreen O'Connor and Mary Lynne Ellis were enormously helpful with their critical contributions and philosophical clarity and this is a far better book than it would have been without their generosity. I also owe much to Judith Summers for her eagle-eyed capacity to spot grammatical errors and her patience in having to deal with so many of them. Pippa Weitz's editorial capacity to be flexible but ultimately unwaveringly firm when it came to my deadline avoidance was also much appreciated.

My thanks go to Ian Birrell and Louisa Saunders who green-lighted my *Independent* column all those years ago, and also to Richard Cook for letting me use his work on the front cover. My thanks also to The Champernowne Trust for making it possible for me to work with people who could not otherwise afford therapy.

Huge thanks to my friends and family for their encouragement, especially to my husband, Richard, who helped me realise that it is possible to get the angel out of the house (for a while at least) and to my sons, Tom, Joseph, and Patrick, who continually remind me, simply by being themselves, what it is really all about.

ABOUT THE AUTHOR

Elizabeth Meakins is a psychoanalyst practising in North London. Prior to training she worked in psychiatry as a senior occupational therapist. Elizabeth has always combined working in mental health with writing about it. Some of the columns she wrote for *The Independent*, Tales from the Therapist's Couch, are reproduced throughout this book. Both her writing and her work as a psychotherapist are informed by a creative diversity of psychoanalytic theorising and by her belief that it is the specificity of each person's story, rather than any particular theoretical perspective, that leads the work.

INTRODUCTION

This book is a response to a question put to me years ago when I was a trainee psychotherapist. Asked by a young woman who had been describing her traumatic experience of sexual abuse, her question to me was: "What will you do with my story?"

I will return to the specifics of her story and the way I responded to it in the last chapter, but her words made me think generally as well as specifically about what we, as therapists, "do" with people's stories, and this book is about that wider response. What ideas about psychoanalysis and emotional growth do we bring to the therapeutic relationship? How do we combine our theory-stories with those we encounter in our practice? How do we ensure that our personal story and whatever informs us in our own lives is not imposed on the other intrusively? How do we place ourselves in the complicated and painful process of someone's struggle for change? Is it possible for this relationship to be an equal one?

All of these are the kinds of questions familiar to every psychotherapist as she starts to practice her training. Each of us encounters a bewildering amount of theory and ideas about techniques needed to translate that theory into practice. Each of us has to try and make our own kind of sense of what we do as we gradually develop an understanding of how we work. Each of us will have had moments of wondering what on earth we are doing and why.

My own training was psychoanalytically eclectic and, as I describe in Chapter One, there were times when the comfort of a specific identity was very appealing. As my early practice got underway, I began to feel increasingly like someone who just doesn't know her own mind. In one session I might be thinking of Klein or Winnicott, in another Jung, and in yet another no theory at all would come to mind but maybe some lines from a poem would feel insistent. How could I work with such an inconsistent plethora of associations that were often not only theoretically incompatible but also frequently outside the ken of any analytic framework?

My awareness of this apparent catholicity in approach was vividly brought home to me when, ten years or so ago, I wrote a column for *The Independent* about psychotherapy. In these fictionalised descriptions of the kinds of emotional terrains familiar to any therapist, I was startled to realise just how seemingly disparate and far-flung my own therapeutic responses often were. Many of these columns are included in the extracted stories throughout this book.

Various influences have enabled me to tolerate and even embrace this evident catholicity. One of these has been a phenomenological way of understanding, a way that recognises how each of us is far more complex than all of the theories put together, so no one way of thinking can be more "right" than any other. This approach also recognises how it is the experience that comes from being with a particular individual that determines what drifts to mind, and that psychotherapy is about following that drift rather than any pre-formulated theory.

As will be clear from the following chapters, another significant influence on my own work has been the writings of the psychoanalyst Marion Milner whose personal diaries and clinical writings describe a capacity to be both anchored in psychoanalytic tradition and open to the surprising and the unexpected. Like other analysts in the Independent Group, Milner allows literature and philosophy, as well as psychoanalytic theory, to inform her thinking about her work, insisting that the experience is always bigger than any one formula.

Since writing the columns for *The Independent*, I have been what is rather strangely described as a "resident psychotherapist" for various magazines, and have discovered, somewhat to my surprise, that the process involved in thinking about "problem page" dilemmas has been unexpectedly helpful for my work as a therapist. The need to attend very carefully to the specifics of someone's framed speech has made me aware of how tempting it can be to respond to the language of distress with some formulae of theory, yet how much more fruitful it is when the temptation to bolt elsewhere is avoided. Learning to stay with the question and avoid any theory or pathology in my response has taught me a lot about the challenging necessity of attending to the specifics of each person's story. Many of these issues are taken up and explored in the following chapters in different ways.

Chapter One focuses on the tension in psychotherapy between what I have called Doubts and Certainties. Therapy is about enabling someone to challenge rigid ways of thinking in order to let new life in, but what about ourselves, as therapists? How comfortable are we with the unknowing that is integral to analytic experience? How do we manage the pressure that comes to us from many directions to be the one who is supposed to know? Freud was steeped in a culture of scientific causality and the metaphors of archaeologist and surgeon, which he used to describe the analysts role, are remote from contemporary theory. Yet the danger of defending ourselves with too much formulated knowing, and so encoding our patients within our own language, remains a real concern. As I explore, many people come to therapy precisely because they have already been too confined by a language that is not their own.

Chapter Two is a reflection on what is the cornerstone of all analytic work: the unconscious. We all talk about it and refer to it as pivotal to what we do, but what is it? *Is* it an "it"? Which of the many ways that psychoanalysis uses to describe unconscious processes do we make use of in our work? Freud's theory argued that we should keep our subjective responses out of the analytic relationship; Jung's understanding was always that this was inevitably a dialectical process, and much contemporary theory encourages us to scrutinise and use our own physical as well as emotional and cognitive response during a session. So how do we each respond to the ways unconscious processes necessarily subvert and derail us from the safety of the known? Examples of dreams, symptoms, and transference processes are some of the ways I use to illustrate how unconscious processes manifest themselves within the therapy relationship.

Chapter Three explores the challenge in knowing when privacy is healthy, when problematic, a difficulty which Winnicott writes about so brilliantly. Therapy often helps us feel aware of what we have spent years managing not to think about. For many people being able to communicate this awareness feels deeply empowering. For others, it feels imperative to continue keeping things tightly under wraps from the world of others. When do we, as a therapist, challenge someone's need to be hidden, and when respect their need to not be found? How do we respond to behaviour that is kept secret from others because it is potentially dangerous and destructive, especially when such behaviour develops during the process of therapy? How, in other words, do we distinguish between what is destructive and constructive, and trust that the former can develop into the latter during the process of analytic change?

Chapter Four focuses on the fact that however hidden or separate we may feel from others, we begin life in a state of intense emotional relatedness. Our experience of ourselves is therefore always deeply relational and intersubjective. How we were held, fed, gazed at, and loved as infants will significantly influence how secure or anxious we feel in relation to both ourselves and others and will determine whether we are able to experience others as different from, as well as similar to, ourselves. Our identity will also be deeply influenced by sexual, racial, and socio-cultural factors. The problems many people experience in their relationships often arise when there is no manageable sense of where one person's subjectivity ends and another's begins. Some of the ways we either control others or allow ourselves to be controlled arise as a defence against the unbearable fears that being alone with ourselves can induce. Some of the ways we manage this separation anxiety are illustrated through different stories.

Chapter Five asks why it is that women are so much more concerned with looking after the needs of others than men. Contemporary feminist thinking explains behavioural differences between the sexes as due to girls learning from birth onwards how to prioritise others' needs above their own, and to split off their experiences deemed to be "unfeminine". Many writers have criticised Freud's theorising for being inherently patriarchal, arguing that the language of analysis often colludes with the very ways of speaking that prevent women from expressing their own subjectivity. The usual litany of female maladies—masochism, narcissism, and hysteria—are illustrated through stories of powerlessness, anorexia, and self-harm, and explored as examples of sexual inequality rather than sexual difference. New theories of perversion recognise this issue of sexual inequality, but does our use of psychopathology ever help the patient? Or is pathologising what we do to protect ourselves from engaging with the discomfort of someone's distress?

Chapter Six explores how therapy often begins with a statement of absence or loss ("I feel empty, dead, stuck, lost") in which any "feeling of real" (Winnicott) is too often absent. Therapy often involves enabling someone to challenge and break down some of the unhelpful ways that are being used as a defence against earlier experiences of vulnerability. The process can feel bewildering and chaotic, but often it is from enduring this time of uncertainty and tolerating emotional separateness without the usual props, that a deeper experience of aliveness can emerge. The chapter looks at the parallel track for therapists to this process: how willing are we to endure the chaos and uncertainty of the unknown in our work? How often do we defend ourselves with the illusory projection that we are the ones who know? Do we try to "do" something to peoples' stories, or do we, like many of our patients, allow ourselves to be challenged and changed by the process?

A short note on language

Psychoanalyst, analysts, therapist, psychotherapist, psychoanalytic psychotherapist

I have used these terms intermittently throughout the book as I long ago abandoned the belief that these distinctions explain any real differences between people. I do not think it is the label we carry but who we are in our work that matters. I also resent the power games that can be generated by differences between trainings. My own training enables me to call myself a psychoanalyst and a psychoanalytic psychotherapist, and it sometimes amuses and sometimes irritates me to notice the different responses that each tag evokes. I think this whole area of how we name ourselves is riveted to the problematically patriarchal history that is part of Freud's legacy.

She

I have employed "she" throughout the book for both simplicity and statistical accuracy. As the majority of patients and the majority of therapists are women, it just makes sense.

Patients

I find this a difficult one because of the obvious links to the medical model of dependency and illness. "Patient" has an aura of containment and holding which I do think is appropriate and as analysis is often about learning to tolerate frustration better, I like the pun with patience. I have never felt very comfortable with "clients" as for me it feels too associated with brusquely efficient service providers, and I personally find "analysand" both too clunky and (in my mind anyway) too specifically the prerogative of Jungian analysts.

We, us, them

Throughout the book, I have often identified with both sides of the equation: patient and therapist. This is partly because if we have trained to be a psychotherapist we will have had the experience of being a patient ourselves. Apart from this standard training obligation, there is another reason for this role reversal. I once heard someone say that no-one should ever think about becoming a psychotherapist unless they had experienced deep and difficult emotional pain. Most of us who decided to embark on the journey of becoming therapists did so because we had somehow at some time in our lives become aware of our own emotional pain and found it interesting or painful enough (or both) to want to explore it further. I think that many of the people who come to see a therapist could easily change places with many of us who sit in the therapist's chair.

CHAPTER ONE

Doubts and certainties

> We that don't know our feeling's shape, But only that which forms
> it from outside
>
> —Rainer Maria Rilke

If you're reading this you're likely to know what it feels like both to tell your story to a therapist and to be that therapist as stories are told. This chapter is about some of the ways psychoanalysis encourages us to think about and work with peoples' stories, and some of the pitfalls inherent in those ways. Psychotherapeutic trainings involve us collecting many maps along the way; reference points to use as we try to work out what might be happening and what we are supposed to be doing. We have all got our own collection, influenced by our therapy, training, supervision, the patients we work with, and wider life experiences. We probably share certain frames of reference with each other fairly comfortably and get hot under the collar at the idea of certain others. Respect for, and tolerance of, theoretical differences doesn't feature prominently in the history of psychoanalysis.

Questions for practice

Having others' ideas in mind whilst engaging with someone's story can often help analytic work, but sometimes it hinders. Sometimes we reach for theory like a fireguard to protect ourselves from the naked heat of what can feel too uncomfortable to bear. Then thinking becomes a safety net that tells us we know what we are doing, whereas it is actually getting in the way of experiencing the unique subjectivity of the other person. People are, after all, so much bigger than any theory. Even Freud's.

So how do we manage this tension between what's already formulated and what hasn't yet been formed? How do we work without letting any particular theoretical frame thwart what needs to emerge freely within the therapeutic process? Is it possible to do so?

Marion Milner

As a way into thinking about these issues further I want to look at a paper by Marion Milner, a psychoanalyst who has been an important part of my own internal map. Milner struggles with the tension between doubt and certainty, known and unknown, in all of her writings: it is present in the diaries she wrote in her early twenties, it is a constant thread in her psychoanalytic writings, and she was still challenging and questioning settled ways of thinking up until her death at the age of ninety-four.

A couple of years before she died I interviewed her about her life and work (see Appendix) and was moved and impressed that despite her failing eyesight she was still avidly reading and questioning familiar concepts and theories. At the time of my visit, this highly respected Freudian-trained and Winnicott and Kleinian-influenced woman was reading a book by a Jungian analyst that explored what we mean by masculine and feminine. "I'm still unsure," she said to me cheerfully. "I'm still studying." It was a heartening glimpse of a genuine capacity to be open to diversity in analytic thinking.

Milner: Blake and Job

In 1956 Milner wrote a paper called *The Sense in Nonsense* (Milner, 1956) in which she uses William Blake's illustrations to the Book of Job to think about what happens if we stick too rigidly to certainties.

Her interpretation of Blake's engravings describes a man who, despite leading an exemplary life, feels wretchedly depressed. Job has prided himself on being morally virtuous, and things are not working out the way he expected. Loved ones die, Job's health deteriorates, and there appears to be no light on the horizon. Job becomes depressed and uncharacteristically prone to explosions of anger about the injustice of it all.

Full of panic as well as rage about the state he is in Job looks around for someone to carry the blame, and for a while Satan becomes a useful scapegoat. But splitting his world into rights and wrongs and raging about the unfairness of his lot doesn't bring any relief, in fact it makes things worse. Then when he is in the midst of the bleakest uncertainty and despair and is suffering a breakdown, something unexpectedly shifts. Recognising that the lopsided way he's been living has a lot to do with the despair he is in, Job loosens his grip on his habit of self-righteousness and stops making the other carry his portion of blame.

There follows Job's struggle to come to terms with a side of his nature he had always imagined only belonged to lesser mortals. His painful recognition of what he had denied about himself puts an end to his moral high ground tone, and after a time of wretched confusion we see Job emerging from his depression with an energy that wasn't present at the beginning. This change is illustrated by the difference between the first picture of Job and his family, in which musical instruments are hanging lifelessly in the background, and Blake's later depiction of them now playing music with clear vitality.

The whole sequence of events is about Job enduring an unfamiliar part of his nature, a destructive part of himself that doesn't sit comfortably with the self-image and moral codes he has been living by. Job, both Milner and Blake seem to be saying, has had both the courage and the humility to see that aliveness is about far more than living by hand-me-down moral codes. Aliveness comes from being able to tolerate sickening doubt and uncertainty rather than projecting on to others whatever doesn't fit in with how we like to see ourselves. Only then can we be open to experiences that do not necessarily fit into whatever creed we have been taught to live by.

Clinical relevance

All of this is, of course, the staple diet of psychoanalysis. The consulting room is a space where contemporary Jobs bring the discomfort of

Figure 1.   Plate 1. Job and his Family, illustration from the *Book of Job*, *c.* 1825 (black carbon ink on paper). Blake, William (1757–1827). Fitzwilliam Museum, University of Cambridge, UK. The Bridgeman Art Library.

struggling with what can't be accommodated into familiar frames of reference. The old ways of doing things don't work any more and an unhinging depression and defensive panic about where uncertainty may lead to floods the therapeutic space.

Like Job, many people deal with confusion and uncertainty by trying to find someone or something to blame. The capacity to split our worlds into rights and wrongs and rigidly clutch on to familiar ways of seeing

Figure 2. Plate 21. *Job and his Wife Restored to Prosperity*, illustration from the *Book of Job*, *c*. 1825 (black carbon ink on paper) Blake, William (1757–1827). Fitzwilliam Museum, University of Cambridge, UK. The Bridgeman Art Library.

when feeling insecure, is the stuff of all our lives, past and present. It is the trigger behind playground fights, sibling squabbles, lovers' tiffs, and the tragedy of wars.

Psychoanalytic theories are full of ideas that explore and explain why we retreat into blaming the "other" when we feel uncomfortably out of depth, and how attempts to buffer ourselves with a Job-like holier-than-thou attitude inevitably fails. Freud talked about a return of the repressed, unconscious projection, splitting, and a plethora of other defence mechanisms to explain such behaviour, and of course these terms have been taken up and developed by different theorists in various ways.

Below are two stories that in very different ways echo elements of Job's experience. From very different theoretical bases, both use the language of splitting and projection to explore how we make our emotional worlds smaller when we are confused and afraid. The first story is about a man who, like Job, struggled with a need to be perfect.

Jung: Shadow, splitting and projection

A man in his mid-forties comes to see me because, as he puts it, "I keep finding myself doing and thinking things quite out of kilter with the person I really am." A friend suggested to him he might be having some kind of midlife crisis, and he wants to find out what this entails.

I ask him about himself, and in particular ask him to describe the person he feels he "really" is. What emerges is a thumbnail sketch of someone very decent and upright who selflessly dedicates much time and energy to several good causes. I ask him about the "out of kilter" moments that precipitated his request for a meeting. He looks ashamed. It's difficult, he tells me, to put into words what's been happening. He's always prided himself on being courteous, but recently he's frequently felt irritable and has been uncharacteristically flying off the handle. For instance, he suddenly massively lost his temper with a friend who was staying with him (the same friend who suggested the midlife crisis) simply because this friend had been listening to music instead of offering to help cook. The incident had left him feeling shaken and full of remorse. He wasn't usually out of control like that at all.

He tells me about this friend, and after a few minutes of recollections my patient suddenly tells me that this man actually reminds him of his younger brother, who was always doing things like listening to music instead of helping their mother. This thought of his brother reminds him of the dream he had the night before. "More of a nightmare than dream really as I woke up in a panic. I often have the same one. I'm being chased, and I'm terrified. I don't usually know who I'm running from, but last night I knew it was my brother."

Some words of Jung's come to mind whilst listening to this man: "I would rather be whole than good", and this phrase makes me think of Jung's theory about the Shadow. Some links begin to emerge between these thoughts and what this man appears to be struggling with. As young children, we all learn early on what to show and what to hide in order to gain approval. Every culture and every family has its own particular shopping list of which qualities should be kept, which discarded. Examples of common "shadows" are ruthless financial ambition, sexual (especially homosexual) expression, emotional vulnerability, intellectual hunger, expressions of individuality, displays of anger and selfishness, envy, hate. Whatever it is that wasn't approved of becomes muted and undeveloped, buried well away from our conscious ego. Yet as the process of psychotherapy describes, the unconscious always returns the repressed in one form or another.

This seemed to be what had happened to the man above. The eldest of two brothers, his father had died when he was only eight. His mother often leant upon her eldest for support and the burden of responsibility to make her happy and proud had made him grow up before his time. His younger brother escaped, as younger brothers so often do, from this maternal mantle of expectation and in his teenage years became something of a black sheep, or scapegoat for the family's unlived emotional life.

Until recently, my patient had been successful in maintaining a firm distance between his self-image and his own rejected black sheep side. But now there was suddenly this moody backlash. As the nightmares revealed, the shadow-brother was in hot pursuit, hostile at being rejected for so long. The fact that my patient's self-portrait was of someone so morally upright and good made this Dorian Grey shadow side all the more terrifying. As Jung said, the brighter the light, the stronger the shadow.

Jung believed that accepting and assimilating aspects of one's shadow was an important moral issue. Disowning and disassociating ourselves from whatever makes us feel uncomfortable not only diminishes our own emotional life but leads to our rejected baggage being dumped upon others. He used the terms projection and splitting to describe how we unload on to others aspects of ourselves that don't tally with our self- image. Job's attempt to blame Satan for the crisis he was in is a clear example of this kind of negative projection, as are the judgemental fraternal feelings of the man above.

The process of withdrawing the shadow, says Jung, can throw all our frames of reference and securities into uncomfortable doubt and confusion. Yet, as the man above went on to discover, knowing the worst about ourselves doesn't mean identifying with it or wallowing in it, and it is invariably just what we have been rejecting of and anxious about that we need if we are going to recover a sense of feeling deeply alive.

Klein, Winnicott, and Keats

The next story similarly involves looking at what happens when uncomfortable feelings become intolerable. In this case a chaotic fluctuation between experiencing the world as benign and malign was dependent upon whether the experience of being with others felt accepting or rejecting. This time it is Klein's ideas on splitting and projection, as well as Winnicott and Keats, which came to mind.

A man arrives for a session almost foaming at the mouth in fury. The cause of this outrage is his boss, who had called this patient to task at a public meeting over a badly done piece of work. Although the reprimand was justified, and although this man had previously always been full of praise for his boss, the public nature of the incident cut him to the quick. The blow to ego was considerable and for many months afterwards his boss continued to be demonised. Then one day, my patient received praise from this same boss for some work he had done, and hey presto: all at once he was waxing lyrical about him again.

Far from being an isolated incident, this way of relating was a regular pattern in this man's life. Depending upon whether they had validated or criticised him, friends, lovers, and colleagues were all, like the troops in the Grand Old Duke of York, either up or down. The theory of Melanie Klein describes this way of responding to uncomfortable feelings as splitting: we split our worlds into a reductive but more manageable arena of rights and wrongs when we can't cope with the snowstorm of emotions that accompanies frustration and misunderstanding.

Like Jung (although also unalike in many ways) Klein used the term "projection" (and "projective identification") to describe how we dump on to and into the other all that feels uncomfortable within us. In steadier moments, when we are able to tolerate a welter of confusing feelings without bolting to an over-hasty defence, we achieve what Klein called rather drably the "depressive position". I prefer Winnicott's term for this as the "capacity for concern". It is the place Job seems to have reached at the end of Milner's interpretation. Better than any psychoanalytic terminology is the poet Keats' description of this same emotional state: "What quality," he writes in a letter to his brothers, "when man is capable of being in uncertainties, Mysteries, doubts, without any irritable reaching after fact & reason."

For most of us, there is probably some degree of vacillation between projective splitting and a capacity for concern in our each and every day. Most of us probably know the uncomfortable aftermath of feeling out of kilter with ourselves and our world when we have been too rashly defensive, compared to the mood of well-being that a more reflective response leaves in its wake. What is more difficult is being able to determine which we live by.

Developing a capacity to be in uncertainties without (as Keats put it) irritably reaching for fact and reason is, of course, at the heart of the whole psychoanalytic endeavour. When someone starts therapy they often (like Job) want to be rid of intolerable uncertainty. Whether the conflict appears to be focussed on an external relationship or a more internal difficulty, therapy is reached for as a clarifier, a way of making transparent what feels unendurably murky and opaque.

Yet what actually happens in therapy often mirrors what happens in Job's story, as for many people the experience of analysis turns worlds upside down and replaces fixed ideas with muddle and confusion. If the therapeutic process "works" there is, by the end of it, a return of sureness, but this is very different from the "irritable reaching after fact" kind of certainty often present at the start.

Being open to doubts and uncertainties as a therapist

If analysis is about encouraging people to challenge rigid ways of thinking in order to allow new life in, then what about us, as the therapists? Where are we on the spectrum of defensive certainty versus a capacity to tolerate uncertainties, doubts and mysteries? Most of us have had lengthy and expensive trainings during which we were inundated with a variety of ways to understand our emotional worlds. Which ideas did we choose to keep ticking over, and why? Does our choice of theory say something about our needs, the needs of our patients, or both?

And what about colleagues who work with very different maps? Are we comfortable with having Freud and Jung on the same page (after all, *they* certainly weren't). And when we're not comfortable with differences, how do we respond? Do we (as Job did) project what feels intolerable on to others, splitting our worlds into rights and wrongs because of a paranoid conviction that some of us are more right than others? Do we bypass engaging with differences and try and agree with everyone because we can't cope with conflict? Or can we accept that no one theoretical model is right: different theory resonates with different experience, and being open to diversity can energise, rather than threaten, both clinical work and our profession as a whole.

Sometimes psychoanalysis seems to take itself so seriously that it's difficult to remember (yet absurd that we need reminding) that no aspect of psychoanalytic thinking has a monopoly on the truth; that any theory is always another way of saying what has somewhere already been said.

Winnicott notes this at the start of his paper "Communicating and not communicating" (Winnicott, 1963, p. 179) when he says that if there is any truth in what he describes it will already have been said by the world's poets. Similarly, any analytic description of splitting and projection, be it Freud's, Klein's, Lacan's, or Jung's, is a drop in the ocean of the many poetic and philosophical explorations since the beginning of recorded time on how we divide our worlds into right and wrong.

Take Euripides' play *The Bacchae*: a brutal reminder of how disastrously out of kilter things become when the "other" is seen through the lens of what we have disowned in ourselves. Or Shakesperare's *King Lear*: the tragedy of a father's destructive rage against the world he loves because one of his daughters challenges his narcissistic need for a positive press. Or, on a very different note, Maurice Sendak's *Where The Wild Things Are*: an exquisite illustration of the journey from angry splitting and projection to sweet return and recovery.

Given that psychoanalysis plays such a miniscule part in the many explorations of what we are all about, and given that research often suggests that there is no evidence that one way of thinking is more therapeutically efficacious than another, why does our choice of theory matter so much to us? Why do we so often fight tooth and claw about it? Maybe another way of putting this is to ask: what function does theory serve? And maybe one answer is that it often serves our own, rather than our patients', needs.

I remember, rather shamefacedly, how I began my training clutching a Jungian identikit like a child with her security blanket. I had been bowled over by reading Jung's *Memories, Dreams, Reflections* (Jung, 1964) in my late teens and a few years later started a Jungian analysis. By the time I decided to train I was convinced that Jung was the Holy Grail. I chose a pluralistic training for purely practical reasons. Despite an alarming preponderance of Post-Kleinians and Lacanians I was sure I could keep the Faith and get through unscathed and intact. Luckily, the process of training, supervision, and a different experience of therapy pushed me out of my comfort zone and shot some of my rigid defences to pieces. I can still remember the visceral discomfort, yet curious relief and freedom, in feeling dislodged from almost dogmatic certainty.

I suspect that a lot of theoretical affiliation amongst therapists is autobiographically driven rather than guided by clinical experience, and so the distinction between working with ways of thinking that are personally comfortable and ways that are relevant to a patient's separate subjective needs becomes blurred. The longing to belong and to recognise ourselves in another's language is strong in us all, but if we go tribal on this need and become us and them-ish, we inevitably fall into the trap of defensively splitting, and we behave in ways that our work is supposedly about challenging.

Freud's scientific legacy

Of course at one level this is just history repeating itself. After all, psychoanalysis has always been rife with factional splitting and, as the work itself demonstrates, old habits die hard. Freud himself had a massive need to prove that his ideas were correct and, as his expulsion of Adler and Jung from the elite savage horde when they dared to challenge his thinking on infantile sexuality illustrates, he resisted challenges to his orthodoxy with Job-like elimination of the bad guys.

Freud's belief in the rights ands wrongs of things was rooted in his scientific background and the prevailing culture of rational, objective proof. In Freud's world, the analyst is likened to a surgeon who needs to put aside his own feelings in order to concentrate on the task in hand, and elsewhere to an archaeologist who objectively reconstructs the past from fragments of recovered material (Freud, 1937). The Freudian therapeutic relationship is a one-way process that requires analytic objectivity and neutrality in order to bring hidden life to consciousness (Freud, 1905).

From objectivity to subjectivity and then to now

Today, with decades of hindsight between now and then, it's easy to see the gap between this scientific ideal and the reality of Freud's deeply subjective presence in his work, a presence that often makes him feel like the ghost writer of his patients' stories (Freud, 1918; Spence, 1982; Spence, 1987), and psychoanalytic theory has spent years catching up with what Freud actually did but didn't own doing (Rycroft, 1985).

The image of surgical objectivity has now been replaced by acceptance of the therapist's (inter) subjectivity as a vital part of the analytic process. (Benjamin, 1990). The intention is now less about trying to make sense of whatever can be retrieved from memory, more about attending to what emerges in the here and now. Less on retrieving what was, more on experiencing what is. The factual, noun-like authority of the scientific, mechanistic, and objective that dominated earlier psychoanalytic theory has given way to less clear-edged descriptions of mutuality, receptivity, reverie, intuition.

Neutrality is out and therapy is now a two-person two-way process in which both people are vulnerable to each others' psychic states and during which both are changed in the process (Ogden, 2002). What Jung had been saying years ago about the dialectical and mutually transformative nature of the analytic relationship (Jung, 1957, para. 1) has (as these words of Bollas' illustrate) become part of widespread psychoanalytic theory: "There are two patients within the session and therefore two complementary sources of free association." (Bollas, 1987, p. 202).

On paper, these seismic shifts in the ways we talk about what we do are a challenge to the idea of the analyst as the one who knows. Instead they suggest a relationship between patient and therapist in which both are at some level deeply at sea together. Yet how realistic is this in practice? Don't our trainings inevitably make us feel that at some level we know something the patient doesn't know? Don't our patients need to transfer on to us the hope that we are the ones that know (Lacan, 1977)? How easy is it to (as Bion said) resist the desire to bring our own memory of knowing into the analytic space?

Being seduced by the hunger for the one who knows

We can probably all think of times we have unconsciously hidden behind premature formulations to protect ourselves from the raw and painful mess of someone else's experience. Feeling another's deep distress can trigger our own deep vulnerabilities, and transference interpretations and other formulations can be close-to-hand ways of warding off what feels too uncomfortable to bear.

Having an intense hope transferred on to us that we possess something someone needs (a hope which psychoanalysis both promises and disappoints) can make it even harder to resist speaking from this defended place. I remember one of my training patients asking if I could give her the "formula" she needed. Feeling anxious that I didn't possess this succouring-and-knowing feed, I remember flailing around in my thoughts to try and find something to give her. I remember the relentless discomfort of her blizzard of words and how I tried to protect myself by making sense out of what was happening, a shield of explanation and theory to protect myself from chaos. It was only after I stopped trying to control the experience with various interpretations, and instead became more unobtrusively receptive, that the work began to move on.

In the following passage from *The Hands of the Living God*, Marion Milner's account of her long-term work with her patient, Susan, Milner describes with characteristic candour this need to be on guard against pressure from self and other to fill the gaps with irrelevant formulations that get in the way of what needs to emerge.

> I began to think that before there could be a real change in her there would have to be a change in me—and not only by coming to understand more and giving better interpretations—for slowly I found I had to give up trying so had to provide her with explanations, a giving up which I found difficult, since she was always clamouring for them. Instead I felt I had to learn to wait and watch and let her know that I was there, watching, and not let myself be seduced into this working too hard for her, trying to tell her, put

into words for her, her unconscious preoccupations; because, I came to suspect, if I let myself be so seduced, which I constantly did, it could only put off the moment, perhaps disastrously, of her finding what she herself had got ... I found myself constantly swinging between the sense of the compulsion to feed her with attempted "good" verbalisations of what I thought she was unconsciously feeling, and the sense, more profoundly felt but too often and too easily lost sight of, that I must stick to trying to direct her attention to the various ways which she was preventing her own creative forces from getting to work on the problem ... Bit by bit I came to see that the theme of being able to tolerate empty-headedness was becoming perhaps crucial in Susan's analysis.

(Milner, 1988, p. 42)

What strikes me as so important here is Milner's recognition that working too hard to be the one who knows, sabotages Susan's capacity to find what she has already unknowingly got. Milner wasn't the first to express this concern. Coltart (1986), Balint (1986), and Ogden (2002) are just some of the many who have written about the danger of stealing a patient's creativity by swamping them with too much formulated knowing. Bion was so aware of the hazards of this potential theft that before starting his analysis with Klein he was reputed to have told her he wanted to remain his own person (Symington, 1996). Certainly, the capacity of Kleinian patients to produce good-bad breast material and Jungian analysands to come up trumps with archetypal dreams suggests that rather than both persons being changed by the process, the analyst is at risk of ghost-writing the patient's story.

The trauma of being defined by another's language

There is a deeply uncomfortable irony in all of this, as many of those who start analysis do so because of their experience of being defined by someone else's language, an experience Khan describes as cumulative trauma (Khan, 1963). Often they have been blown about like thistledown by others' impingements and are not free to hear their own voice, to experience their own subjectivity. The following poem by a fourteen-year-old boy is a harrowing and haunting expression of this kind of impingement.

He always
He always wanted to explain things but no one cared.
So he drew.

Sometimes he would draw and it wasn't anything.
He wanted to carve it in stone or write it in the sky.
He would lie out on the grass and look up at the sky and it would be
Only the sky and the things inside him that needed saying.

And it was after that that he drew the picture.
It was a beautiful picture. He kept it under his pillow and would let no one see it.
And he would look at it every night and think about it.
And when it was dark and his eyes were closed he could see it still.
And it was all of him and he loved it.

When he started school he brought it with him.
Not to show anyone, but just to have it with him like a friend.

It was funny about school.
He sat in a square brown desk like all the other square desks and he thought
it would be red.
And his room was a square brown room, like all the other rooms.
And it was tight and close. And stiff.

He hated to hold the pencil and chalk, with his arm stiff and his feet flat on the floor, stiff, with the teacher watching and watching.

The teacher came and spoke to him.
She told him to wear a tie like all the other boys.
He said he didn't like them and she said it didn't matter.

After that they drew. And he drew all yellow and it was the way he felt about morning. And it was beautiful.
The teacher came and smiled at him. "What's this?" she said, "Why don't you draw something like Ken's drawing?
Isn't it beautiful?"

After that his mother bought him a tie and he always drew aeroplanes and rocket ships like everyone else.

And he threw the old picture away.
And when he lay out alone looking at the sky, it was big and blue and all of everything, but he wasn't any more.

He was brown and square inside and his hands were stiff.
And he was like everyone else. All the things inside him that needed saying didn't need it anymore.

It had stopped pushing. It was crushed,
Stiff.

Like everything else.

(Anon)

Many people come to analysis with this experience of emptiness, loss, theft. Sometimes, as illustrated in the two examples below, there is a known cause, a loved villain who whether situational or personal, is understood as having in some way caused the theft.

A man begins therapy by identifying himself as both homosexual and Roman Catholic. He feels unable to be both a practicing homosexual and a practicing Roman Catholic because the letter of the Church Law and the priests he has confessed to tell him that it is a sin, a mortal sin, to physically practice his sexuality. For many years he vacillates between living out his sexual desire and switching back to celibacy in a guilt-ridden U-turn of compliance with Church Law. Caught between a savage rejection of his subjective language and a hunger to be accepted by the objective language of the Church he loves, he is caught in an unbearable double-bind of suffering.

A woman always talks about herself in the plural. The "I" is always the "we" because she has never experienced herself as existing separately from her mother. Every possible decision in her life is scrutinised under the microscope of what her mother might think of it. As the likely outcome is usually negative, decisions of any sort are few and far between. Before starting therapy she had spent long days of long months hiding under her duvet, afraid of answering the phone, afraid to venture into life because her capacity to engage with her world with any vital and potent sense of self had become sapped before conscious memory began.

Mostly the experience of being engulfed by someone else's language is less clear-cut, and there is no clear external object, no Mother Church or biological Mother, to make sense of what is being hidden from. The experience of loss is described less as a battle against something or someone, more as generalised impotence and uncertainty. The story below is a reflection on this kind of cumulative life-sapping indecisiveness.

A man in his late thirties lies slouched in the chair opposite me. He looks perplexed. "I just don't know," he says in a rueful tone. "I mean, she's nice, really nice. I don't want to lose her. But I don't know that I want to commit myself to anything more serious. At the moment, anyway. Who knows, the right woman may be waiting round the corner." Far from being limited to either a specific woman or his romantic life in general, this mood of uncertainty has become the hallmark of who he is, the lens through which he peers at all life decisions, and the agony of never knowing what he really wants in life is what brought him to therapy in the first place.

Chronic indecisiveness has often been cited as a form of insanity, not the madness of the locked wards but a form of madness which can easily be found in the minds and lives of the normative and successful. There is a section in Kierkegaard's The Sickness Unto Death in which he explores the agony of this state of mind. He describes the seductive but essentially dangerous appeal of living in a world of endless and indecisive possibility: "Possibility appears to the self ever greater and greater, more and more things become possible, because nothing becomes actual. At last it is as if everything were possible—but this is precisely when the abyss has swallowed up the self. What is really lacking," he writes, "is the power to submit to the necessary in oneself."

"The necessary in oneself": what does he mean by that? For me, the term calls to mind the words of Gerard Manley Hopkins in his exquisite poem As Kingfishers Catch Fire: "... myself it speaks and spells, crying what I do is me, for that I came."

Whatever one's own associations to the term, it is the immediate, often floundering, lack of the necessary in oneself that is behind many people's venture into therapy. Like the young man above, many people feel they have lost some inner bearing. They describe how they move through their lives full of self-doubt, uncertain about their capacity to make the right choices or commitments. Sometimes, like the young man above, their chronic indecisiveness is masked by a very busy lifestyle. Yet although busy, sometimes frenetically busy, their activity is steered by external currents and they frequently describe moods of emptiness, numbness. Everything exists on the same plane of feeling, and there is a noticeable lack of spontaneity or desire behind the whirlwind of activity.

Although superficially poles apart from restless activity, chronic indecisiveness also frequently reveals itself through inertia. A young woman with whom I once worked became engulfed by a terrible lethargy. She found it impossible to make her mind up about the simplest of things. Nothing awoke her because nothing seemed to contain any meaning or desire. Fortunately, she began after a while to become aware of, and interested in, her unconscious processes, her hidden, neglected life. Remembering her dreams was one manifestation of this. Trains and train stations figured frequently in her dream language and she would invariably wake up to the frustration of having missed yet another journey. The meaning was a clear as day. She needed to get on board, catch her own train. Hooked by the challenge of her own dream life she began to consciously address and wake up the "necessary" in herself. Beneath her lethargy was an extremely strong will. She had become afraid, in a way, of her own power and purpose and she became bravely open to challenging a self-identification that had become stultifying and restricting. About a year after we had finished working together I received a postcard: "… thought you might be amused to know that in last night's dream I finally caught that train!"

It is impossible to generalise why someone struggles with chronic indecision. We all learn to identify with ways of thinking which are not our own, and fairly early on we probably all learn to hide and doubt the difference and difficulty of our own desires. As we grow older it often becomes less and less easy to know what it is that we really want. The capacity to locate what makes us feel deeply and authentically alive can feel remote and unavailable.

Indecisiveness can often be about a loss of connection with what Winnicott calls "the feeling of real" (Winnicott, 1956, p. 304), and when someone who is experiencing this absence comes to therapy they frequently look to the analyst to tell them what to do with their story. The dangers of succumbing to this pressure and impinging on someone's emotional space with premature formulations has been explored above, but what hasn't been answered is the question which this chapter started with: how do we make sure that we get the right balance between the known and the unknown in the therapeutic process? How do we stop ourselves from repeating the experience that brings many to therapy in the first place by eclipsing emerging subjectivity with our pre-formulated ways of seeing?

The figure of Prospero comes to mind. Prospero, the main protagonist in Shakespeare's play *The Tempest*, uses the power of his books and the theories he gleans from them to control the behaviour of all who visit his island-space. The lack of equality between him and the other characters is clear: they are under his thrall. He is the one who knows, the one who holds the power. Then at the end of the play something extraordinary happens. Prospero tires of this omnipotence and omniscience, he tires of it because he realises this way of doing things sets him apart from those around him. He wants a different kind of intimacy. He wants to be on equal footing. But to make this change he has to throw away his technique, his books, his power.

Is it possible or desirable for therapists to, like Prospero, throw away the power that potentially divides us from each other and our patients? Is it possible to do what Bion recommends and really leave our theories out of our relationship with our patients and each other? What would we be left with? As Phillips asks in *Equals*: what would a psychoanalysis be like that recognised and legitimised different voices rather than one that continually implies, if not imposes, the "right" way of thinking? (Phillips, 2002).

In both Prospero's and Job's stories the giving up of their power-laden ego-identifications is simultaneous with letting something else in, some unlived, previously rejected, life. In his final speech Prospero calls upon the world beyond his immediate control to help him on his way, whilst Job's capacity to trust the unknown in himself is illustrated by his playing of the musical instruments that had been gathering dust at the start. By letting themselves become less defended, they both become more empowered because less rigidly powerful.

The playing of musical instruments as an image of recovery resonates with Winnicott's belief that "therapy is about bringing the patient from a state of not being able to play to being able to play" (Winnicott, 1974, p. 44). For Winnicott, playing is synonymous with trusting unconscious processes, trusting that there is a force within us that can be hampered by fears and doubts but which essentially makes for growth.

The next chapter is about this force which makes for growth. We are used to talking about the unconscious. It is the cornerstone of analytic therapy. Dreams, reveries, body language, and whatever we mean by transference, are some of the ways we look for and describe manifestations of it, whilst symptoms are always a sign that some disturbing experience has been responded to with fear.

But what do we *really* mean by the unconscious? And what about our own part in that story? How much does our relationship with our own unconscious processes shape what goes on, or doesn't, in therapy? How much, in other words, is the process of change in a patient (the shift from musical instruments gathering dust to having them played with vitality) dependent on our own aliveness and trust in the unknown?

References and suggested reading

Anon. Poem by a 14 year old boy. Every attempt has been made to source this poem which has been widely published elsewhere.

Balint, M. (1986). The Unobtrusive Analyst. In: G. Kohon (Ed.), *The British School of Psychoanalysis, the Independent Tradition*. London: Free Association Books.

Benjamin, J. (1990). Recognition and destruction: An outline of intersubjectivity. In: S. Mitchell & A. Aron (Eds), *Relational Psychoanalysis, the Emergence of a Tradition*. Hillsdale, NJ: The Analytic press, 1999.

Bion, W. R. (1970). *Attention and Interpretation* (Reprinted London: Karnac, 1984).

Bollas, C. (1987). *The Shadow of the Object: Psychoanalysis of the Unthought Known*. London: Free Association Books.

Coltart, N. (1986). Slouching Towards Bethlehem. In: G Kohon (Ed.), *The British School of Psychoanalysis, the Independent Tradition*. London: Free Association Books.

Freud, S. (1905). A Case of Hysteria. *S.E.*, *7*, London: Hogarth Press.

Freud, S. (1918). An Infantile Neurosis. *S.E.*, *17*, London: Hogarth Press.

Freud, S. (1937). Constructions in Analysis. *S.E.*, *23*, London: Hogarth Press.

Jung, C. G. (1957). Principles of Practical Psychotherapy. In: *The Practice of Psychotherapy*, C. W. 16 (trans. H. G. Baynes). London: Routledge, 1993.

Jung, C. G. (1964). *Memories, Dreams, Reflections*. London: Routledge & Kegan Paul.

Khan, M. (1963). The concept of cumulative trauma. In: *The Privacy of the Self*. London: Hogarth Press, 1974.

Lacan, J. (1977). *The Four Fundamental Concepts of Psycho-Analysis*. London: Hogarth. (Reprinted London: Penguin, 1991).

Milner, M. (1956). The sense in nonsense (Freud and Blake's *Job*). In: *The Suppressed Madness of Sane Men*. London: Tavistock, 1987. (Reprinted London and New York: Routledge, 1988).

Milner, M. (1988). *The Hands of the Living God*. London: Virago Press.

Ogden, T. H. (2002). *Conversations at the Frontier of Dreaming*. London: Karnac.

Phillips, A. (2002). *Equals*. London: Faber and Faber.

Rilke, R. M. (1978). *Duino Elegies* (trans. and eds. Leishman, J. B. & Spender, S.). London: Chatto & Windus.

Rycroft, C. (1985). *Psychoanalysis and Beyond*. London: Chatto and Windus.

Spence, D. P. (1982). *Narrative Truth and Historical Truth*. London and New York: W. W. Norton and Company.

Spence, D. P. (1987). *The Freudian Metaphor*. London and New York: W. W. Norton and Company.

Symington, J. N. (1996). *The Clinical Thinking of Wilfred Bion*. London and New York: Routledge.

Winnicott, D. W. (1956). Primary maternal preoccupation. In: *The Maturational Process and the Facilitating Environment*. London: Hogarth Press, 1965. (Reprinted London: Karnac, 1990).

Winnicott, D. W. (1963). Communicating and not communicating leading to a study of certain opposites. In: *The Maturational Process and the Facilitating Environment*. London: Hogarth Press, 1965. (Reprinted London: Karnac, 1990).

Winnicott, D. W. (1974). *Playing and Reality*. London: Penguin.

CHAPTER TWO

Learning to be in the dark

> When I do truly believe, from continual experience, in a "creative
> unconscious" ... why the fight against it? ... why is it so difficult to
> say: "over to you"?
>
> —Marion Milner

All analytic work is essentially, vitally, an act of trust in the unconscious, a statement of belief that we are lived by more than consciousness. As therapists we often bandy the term unconscious
about like a familiar, a known, a thing. Yet what do we understand by
it? And is it an "it"? How is it possible to talk about what is by definition unknowable, unplumbable?

Freud

Freud's way of describing what was the cornerstone of his new science
shape-changed (as did so many of his ideas) over time. He used the term
unconscious as both noun and adjective (Laplanche & Pontalis, 1973).
When referred to in an adjectival sense, it signifies all that we are not
consciously attending to at any given moment. When it is noun-like

(as it is in so much of his early theory) the unconscious is described as a map; the boundaries between the different states of unconscious, preconscious, and consciousness (or later id, ego, and superego, and primary and secondary processes) delineated like border crossings that can be navigated with the help of one who is (supposed) to know. In Freud's early theory the unconscious is a disturbing terrain (Freud, 1915c). Rather like the opening scenes from *Hamlet*, there is the sense of needing to be continually at watch because fearful of being spooked by encounters from the troubled and troublesome realm of our disquieting past.

In Freud's later theory, psychic life is structured into three "agencies": the id, ego, and superego, and unconscious processes are now mostly described in an adjectival rather than a noun sense (Freud, 1923b). Another change is that unconscious processes are no longer only associated with the id: the unattended parts of the ego and superego are now also described as unconscious.

Although these shifts make Freud's evolving description of unconscious processes feel more dynamic, less reduced to a structural known, Freud's whole *raison* was (as explored in the last chapter) about rational knowing; and so, although he compares his theories of the mind to "areas of colour melting into one another as they are presented by modern artists" (Freud, 1923b, p. 112), it is his tone of rigorous scientific certainty that so often permeates his work.

At his seventieth birthday celebrations, for example, Freud is reputed to have said that although the poets and philosophers discovered the unconscious before him, his unique contribution was the scientific method by which it could be studied (MacIntyre, 1967). In keeping with his Darwinian approach, Freud saw progress as a sort of evolution from unconscious to conscious, unknown to known, or in his own famous words: "Where id was there ego shall be" (Freud, 1923b, p. 112). In this quest for rational certainty the fixed noun sense of things carries more weight than adjectival fluidity.

Jung

Jung's take on the unconscious was always significantly different from Freud's. He thought there is a collective, as well as personal, aspect to unconscious processes, and his belief that libido is energy with a more than specifically sexual function led to his rupture with Freud. In Jung's description, the unconscious depicts an extremely fluid state of affairs: everything of which I know, but of which I am not at the moment thinking; everything of which I was once conscious but have now forgotten; everything perceived by my senses, but not noted by my conscious mind; everything which, involuntarily and without paying attention to it, I feel, think, remember, want and do; all the future things that are taking shape in me and will sometime come to consciousness: all this is the content of the unconscious.

(Jung, 1991a, para. 382)

Phenomenology

Phenomenology attends to descriptions of the immediacy of lived experiences rather than explanations. Challenging the dualisms of inner/outer, mind/body, conscious/unconscious, thinkers like Merleau-Ponty (Merleau-Ponty, 2002) and Levinas (O'Connor, 2010) view the unconscious as co-extensive with, rather than distinct from, consciousness. Their attention to the essential intersubjectivity of our life (the fact that our sense of self emerges from a particular socio-cultural as well as familial context) has far-reaching implications for how we think about and work with unconscious processes (an area further explored in Chapters Four and Five).

Marion Milner

Milner's understanding of unconscious processes developed into something with a greater purpose and potential than Freud's. Through her interest in artists' descriptions of their creative processes, her own life experience, and her clinical work, she came to understand analysis as a space that enables us to trust in "the mysterious force by which one is lived, the 'not self' which was yet also in me" (Milner, 1986, p. 179). Therapy is about enabling someone to explore and develop what is unconsciously already present and known. Milner's shift in thinking was influenced by Winnicott's ideas and echoed by what other analysts in the Independent group were discovering and expressing.

Bion

Bion similarly emphasises the positive importance of unconscious processes as the route to development, and, in a significant departure from Freud's theory, his ideas about reverie and intuition make the therapist's use of her own unconscious processes integral to the work. Bion believed that an inability to tolerate frustration and uncertainty was the biggest block to a capacity for creative thought and growth, and that therapy challenges us to tolerate "multiple vertices" (Bion, 1984)— different perspectives on something or someone at any one time.

Lacan

For Lacan, the unconscious is structured like a language (Evans, 1996; Lacan, 1977) and we are made aware of this language through slips of the tongue, dreams, and other expressions of what has been repressed. The aim of analysis is not to make the unconscious conscious, as the unconscious is neither internal nor reducible. Analysis is about challenging "empty speech" and enabling the discovery of "full speech" through an acceptance of lack (castration) and our mortality.

Relevance for us today

After that glance at some of the ways unconscious processes have been explored and explained in recent history, some of Meltzer's words come to mind: "The thrust of psycho-analysis has moved relentlessly from a simplistic explanatory hypothesis and an optimistic aim to cure mental illness, towards a state of bewildered description of mental phenomena" (Meltzer, 1992, p. 3). How does each of us navigate this bewilderment and what do we translate from it into our own work and understanding?

Whatever the differences in our theoretical approaches, most therapists recognise the experience of dreams, symptoms, associations, and transference phenomena as ways of working with the unconscious. Below I give examples of each of these, to explore how unconscious processes are part of what happens during therapy. Separating out the ways by which we become aware of these processes is inevitably reductive as they continually merge and overlap.

Dreams

Dreams have a life of their own outside of the therapeutic space. The products of another's intrapsychic activity, they exist before we (as either patient or therapist) consciously encounter them. Freud once wrote that psychoanalysis was about learning to see in the dark, and dreams come from that place of dark. They are, of course, shaped into language by the dreamer and again shape-changed during the process of therapy, but however much they are altered through the conversations that happen around and about them, a dream always has its own contour, its beginning, middle, and end that was cooked up in the unconscious before it became remembered and shared.

This sense of a dream hatching beyond our conscious control makes the dreaming world close to how writers often describe the process of creating. The following reflection by the artist Partou Zia describes the poetic process, but she could just as easily be describing the experience of a dream: "But you know, poetry is a secret process. Its gestation can take place only when all is dark. The unknown and the voiceless. Unknowing in the sense of the strange, the curious sense of being unknown even to oneself. Time slips in and Time slips out" (Zia, 1994).

So how do we respond to dreams, our own or those of a patient? Do we understand them as a return of the repressed, or the arrival of something new? How do we decide which of our own associations we put into the pot? The following piece is based on a dream that a woman in her early twenties brought to a session.

> "Last night I dreamed I gave birth to a dead baby. I also dreamed I was standing by some water, and at my feet was a fish, gasping for air, dying on the ground."
>
> Dreams. We all have them, although we may rarely remember them. They erupt into our waking life, leaving us with images of strangeness and intensity that gradually dissolve into our daytime worlds.
>
> For Freud, dreams were the royal road to the unconscious, a pathway into that huge sea of the unknown and unexpressed. Audible in everyday jokes and slips of the tongue, becoming problematic if struggled with in phobias or panic attacks, expressions from the unconscious are always a reminder that we are lived by more than our conscious worlds.
>
> The images above were dreamed by a young woman. She first came to see me heavy with an unhappiness she couldn't make sense of. The burden was literal as well as emotional. She was

very overweight. She described how she fed herself continually as if trying to satiate some terrible emptiness.

For many weeks it was difficult to get a sense of who she was. I often felt wooden, empty in her presence. Nothing in the analytic space was stirring. Because things felt so stuck I asked her if she ever remembered her dreams. One day soon after this she brought the above images to a session. As she spoke them out, their truth startled her. She did feel, she admitted, very much like a fish out of water. She hadn't dreamed on purpose, but there seemed to be a purpose in the dreams. Some energy somewhere inside of her started to kick into life.

Over the next five years I was both part of and witness to the unfolding of a deeply moving process. Two or three times a week she would sit in my room, incredulous at the wealth of dream material she was discovering in herself. At first her dreams were littered with the hungry, dead, and dying. Bits of bodies scattered across some landscape, more dead babies. I am often surprised how frequently people experience dismemberment dreams. Why, in the depths of sleep, does psyche come up with such horrific images? What do the lifeless scattered fragments say about the dreamer's state? As so often with frequently occurring dream motifs, these images are present in ancient stories. From Humpty Dumpty to Osiris and the Bacchae, there are mythical stories of bodies being broken into bits, scattered, and sometimes magically reassembled.

With the re-membering of the dreams began the task of under-standing the symptoms that had been deadening her life. Her mother had become pregnant again when she was only a few weeks old, and breast-feeding had abruptly stopped. When she was only seven months old her sister was prematurely born, and had taken up much of her mother's time and care. Experienced as brighter, more beautiful and more extrovert than she was, her sister had been a source of envy for as long as she could remember.

Her desperate hunger now began to make sense, as did the dreams of lifelessness and dismemberment. These images of cut off and neglected parts of the self seemed to reflect how she had felt for so many years, and how I had experienced her in the early months of our work together. Constant comparison and self-criticism meant that she had never been able to live her potential. But as time went on, and she consciously began to challenge her ceaseless self-negation, she started to appear as herself within the dreams, often as a vet-like figure nursing wounded animals. This stirred a sense of hope, and gradually, very slowly, bit by bit, she began to respond differently to the tidal waves of need that had been over-whelming her and had brought her to therapy in the first place.

Like a gift from the gods her discovery of her inner life made her realise just how cut off from both herself and the world around her she had been for so long. No longer hungry for a life always elsewhere, she was becoming aware of her own sense of self. She stopped eating her heart out, gradually lost a lot of weight, and, like an animal emerging after long hibernation, roused herself for her own life. And then one day, near the end of her analysis, she dreamed she gave birth to a healthy baby girl.

Of course, dreams are not essential to analytic work, but are invaluable when the conscious self has become rigidly closed to the unknown. There is no dream dictionary, no right interpretation. Dreams are like our own pieces of poetry, our particular life forces struggling to be realised.

The dream came from this woman, not me, but in mulling it over together we were both part of how it took on a different shape. I told her some of my thoughts, had a hand in influencing the way we viewed it. Did my interventions steal the dreaming experience from her, or enrich it? Did talking about it reduce it to an interpreted world and so rob it of its continual and vital mystery? Did I respond to her expectation that I know about these things by reaching for meaning too soon? Should we reach for meanings at all (Khan, 1989)? Does being seen as the one who knows about things unconscious get in the way of the rich complexity of our experience (Phillips, 1995)? There are no answers, only questions about what Ogden has called the conversations that take place at the frontiers of dreaming (Ogden, 2002).

Symptoms and internal conflicts

Phobias, obsessions, compulsions, blushing, stammering, addictions, eating disorders, depression. Like dreams, symptoms signify the pres-ence of unconscious processes, but unlike dreams they are the outer signs of turmoil between our conscious and unconscious selves, the post- invasion security locks we rig up because some unexpected intrusion has made us uncomfortably aware that we are not as safely in control as we would like to be.

The problem with symptoms is that they never carry an expiry date, but like some malfunctioning lighthouse that signals warnings of dangerous seas when the waters have become calmer, our bodies live in continual expectation that whatever disturbed us will return again.

Why we learned to feel the way we do becomes the question taken up in therapy. What happened to make us retreat in anxiety and fear? Or did we learn to approach our worlds with an expectation of danger, an anticipatory, rather than reactive, anxiety and fear? Whichever way it is, or was, analytic work slowly shifts symptoms by enabling us to think about why we started to do things the way we do. The process enables us to loosen and detach ourselves from habitual defences and discover a better way of dealing with life when turmoil comes our way.

Cognitive behavioural versus psychoanalytic therapy

Something of an unnecessary Cold War often exists between psychodynamic and cognitive behavioural therapies, unnecessary because often, especially with phobic, obsessive, and compulsive symptoms, a cognitive and behavioural approach can be an indispensible part of early work. Sometimes people are so consumed by the distress of battling with a symptom that focussing on specific objectives in a very concrete non- analytic way is where they clearly want to start. Often the feeling of empowerment from managing to feel in control of, rather than controlled by, "it", however fractionally, loosens things up and shifts an immobilising despair so that deeper exploratory unravelling can begin.

An agoraphobic woman needs her partner to be with her before she can leave the house, and her shame in this dependency figures heavily in our conversations. She longs to change this debilitating neediness, and we explore how she thinks she could do so. She sets herself the task of walking around the block by herself every day before our next session and she is triumphant at managing four times out of six.

A deeply depressed man who has spent many long days of the last few months hidden under his duvet rarely manages to get to therapy. I am charging him for missed sessions, which provokes no reaction until one day he is uncharacteristically furious about the invoice.

As is so often the case with furies, a new energy becomes available in our conversations. As well as the injustice about being charged for something he can't help doing, he is angry with his listless, lifeless state. He wants to fight it, to catch it out. The conversation includes talk of setting traps. He says he will place the alarm out of reach on a loud ringing tone that will irritate his flatmates, and when they thump on the wall he will try to get out of bed to turn it off. The anger has now become an envious attack on those who don't suffer like him. After two months he manages to stay up almost every weekday after it has rung.

Conflicts: terminable or interminable?

Early conversations in therapy are often dominated by a kind of battlefield progress report on the advance or retreat of symptoms (did the fight against giving in to a compulsion or addiction, or the struggle to say yes rather than no when day breaks, succeed?). The following words, from a woman who struggled with compulsive eating, illustrate this early kind of preoccupation.

> I fell at the first hurdle last night. Went straight to the fridge when I got in from work. Had had such a shit day. More than anything in the world I just want to stop this binge eating. I hate myself for it so much. I've managed to keep it under control for up to a month before now. It's when I'm stressed, the strain of not giving into that urge to stuff my face is huge. I'm so tired of this battle, this endless fight for self-control. I'd give anything to feel free of it. I suppose I was once free of it, as a child. It's difficult to remember any time when I was without it.

Like the woman in the first story, her energy was consumed by her ceaseless, tiring, demoralising battle with food. Other people's battles are often similarly object fixated; the desire to quit door-checking, drinking, drugs, or a love affair, conflicts with the equally strong desire to check the lock one more time, pour a drink, get a line of coke, make the illicit phone call. Like many people with a specific fight on their hands she had the fantasy that if her insatiable need for food could be exorcised, all would be sorted and life would be conflict free and manageable.

Whether the battle is focussed on an external object or is described as more inward and existential (the conflict, for example, between the person we'd like to be and the person we often become, or between the seemingly incompatible desires of our many selves) this longing to find resolution and truce is often expressed by those struggling with inner turmoil. So how do we as therapists respond to this longing to be conflict free?

Conflict resolution or irresolution?

At one level, Freud's whole body of work is built upon the notion of conflict resolution: where id was, there ego shall be. The ego's colonisation of the problematic id implies that victory in the average neurotic civil war is possible. Yet as well as hallmarking his work with the id versus ego conflict resolution image, Freud also describes the ongoing and unresolvable battle within us all between Eros and Thanatos, life and death, hope and despair, as a quintessentially human and inevitable experience of conflict.

The next piece, loosely based on Freud's id, ego, and superego hat trick, is about this inevitability of internal inconsistency. Based on two very different experiences of guilt, it illustrates how understanding and accepting the confusion of inner turmoil (rather than trying to hide from or defeat it) can enable us to feel strengthened and enlivened by the challenging complexity of ourselves. (The idea that therapy can enable us to feel comfortable with, and even enjoy, internal contradiction is explored more fully in Chapter Six).

> A woman who has been having weekly therapy for several months describes what she calls her thought battle: "There's the bossy voice imposing what I have to do, and the angry, anxious one just wanting to be left in peace." This internal battle causes all decision-making to be emotionally exhausting. My patient describes deciding not to go to a colleague's party due to tiredness, then being unable to enjoy the free time because of feeling crippled with guilt. Similarly, a decision not to visit her mother one weekend led to hours of anguish.
>
> After a few sessions it is clear that one word rings out louder than any other in her sessions. It is guilt. A constant internal warfare between "wants" and "oughts" is causing her to feel debilitated with guilt about the most mundane of things.

A man in his early twenties comes to therapy with a specific agenda. He has just completed his first year as a medical student and is feeling deeply unhappy. He tells me that for as long as he can remember he has wanted to be a writer, but his family treated this notion as an adolescent whim and assumed he would continue the family tradition of working in medicine. The pressure to do so was particularly strong from his father, so the young man buckled down and towed the line. But one year on, he knew he had made a huge mistake. He had done badly in the end of year exams, partly because his time and energy was being poured into a novel he was currently writing. An editor had shown some interest, and he realised he couldn't go on any longer trying to please his father.

He came to see me laden with guilt about hurting those he loved, but knowing that if he didn't follow his own heart he would be a lesser, sadder man. To "save himself" he had to risk disappointing his parents. What he wanted from therapy was a space where he felt understood and accepted, to help him manage the burden of guilt as he made his announcement and change.

Guilt: both of the above patients were suffering from it, yet in very different ways. We talk about guilt as gnawing, immobilising, and crippling, but what exactly is it? The dictionary defines it as "a painful feeling of self reproach resulting from the sense that that one has done something wrong." Freud described it as painful internal warfare between the id, the ego, and the superego. The id represents our unlived, unexpressed, and chaotically instinctive experience. The superego refers to the suppressive part of ourselves which we internalise fairly early on from parents and teachers, revealing itself through chastising thoughts which curb our instincts. Squashed between these conflicting emotions sits the ego, trying to cope with and negotiate the discomfort of this battle.

Depending upon the kind of authority we internalised as children, our experience of guilt will be either healthy or neurotic. If much of our sense of what is right and wrong was learned in an atmosphere of fear, then the guilt we experience from the conflict between our expressive and suppressive sides is likely to be neurotic. If it was learned with love and understanding, our guilt will be a healthy if painful part of growing up: a wrestling with the conscience more than with the superego, and a capacity to accept that we are bound to sometimes hurt those we love but that we must articulate and sometimes act upon our impulses all the same.

The woman above was paralysed by neurotic guilt. As the only child of an unhappy marriage, her mother's energy went into controlling her, as if to do so might ease her pain. My patient remembered constantly feeling that she was always doing the wrong thing. During her teenage years she began to fight back, becoming an exaggeration of the wilful character that her mother feared. Then, after she had left home, the mother she had unwittingly internalised began to once again dominate her life in the form of a harsh superego, chastising and restricting her spontaneity at every turn.

The young man, on the other hand, highlights a constructive way of dealing with a healthy sense of guilt. Separating from our families and becoming the person we feel ourselves to be causes most people some degree of conflict and anguish. If, as in the case of this young man, we don't let guilt either hamper us from doing what feels deeply right or blame those who we feel have made us feel guilty in the first place, we can channel internal conflict into something more constructive: a conscience which balances loving concern for others with the need to live according to our subjective understanding of the rights and wrongs of things.

Transference processes

The terms transference and countertransference are so overloaded with a complicated history of meanings and an almost esoteric expectation of psychic phenomena, that this area more than any other is, I think, where theoretical explanations and expectations can block us from experiencing what is actually happening. I can remember as a trainee trying to think of an example of transference during a seminar and feeling like someone in *The Emperor's New Clothes*, trying to persuade myself that I could see something that was not really there. I remember my relief at coming across a paper by Roderick Peters (Peters, 1991) which explores how sometimes the transference hits you between the eyes but at other times, because transference can happen in all significant relationships, outside as well as inside therapy, this projection is not always strongly present.

Here (as elsewhere in this book) I use the term transference to describe how a patient often unconsciously relates to her therapist as someone significant from the past. Usually, but not always, this is a parent or sibling, and, of course, as the nature of any relationship is variable both during one time and over time, a mother, or father, can be experienced as malign and benign in the same minute, let alone the same fifty-minute hour. I also work with a belief that what is "transferred" can often be an expression of fundamentally new experiences, so a facilitation of the unlived *in potentia* that is within us all.

What does transference feel like?

Breaks, especially unexpected ones, often awaken early abandonment and attachment issues and so inevitably produce strong transference responses. I experienced a clear example of this a while ago when I had to cancel work unexpectedly for two weeks for personal reasons. I hadn't told patients why I had needed to cancel sessions, and when I returned to work the diversity of response to my unexplained absence was striking.

One woman believed I had cancelled her sessions because I just couldn't bear to be in the room with her any longer. Her experience of her mother was of someone immensely critical and rejecting who continually threatened to abandon her if she didn't do what she was told.

Another patient vented unstoppable fury at me for not having been there for him: my name, he told me, had been dirt in his house during my absence. As a child, he had never had the experience of being deeply heard, emotionally recognised, and had spent his life looking desperately, hungrily, and angrily for the mirroring he had lacked.

Another patient said, very quietly, that I had never before cancelled and she felt sure that I had been absent for a bereavement and she wanted me to know that she was sorry for that. She had been born prematurely and, as is often the case with people born too early, she had developed intensely empathic intuition, as if the experience of being traumatically separated from the body of the mother she had hungered for had made her antennae finely tuned to the emotional world of those she was so needy of.

Finally, one patient who hadn't developed any strong attachment to me, and who was very resistant to letting himself feel any dependence on or need for anyone, said that it had been something of a relief to have time out. This man had lived in numerous care and foster homes since the age of six and had learned how to avoid feeling emotionally needy of anyone.

Countertransference

Countertransference is usually described as our unconscious response to a patient's presence (what we feel physically and emotionally and which thoughts come to mind). This does not mean that everything we feel and think during a session needs to be interpreted as being about a patient's psychopathology and unconscious processes. If we do that we fail to recognise how our own emotional disturbances are embedded in and often triggered by what's being talked about. It also prevents us from allowing what can be a very real but non transference-based relationship from developing (Greenson, 1972, Szasz, 1963).

The third space: Ogden and the Relational School

In any therapy session there is a complex interchange between two subjectivities. Both people in the room have "their own thoughts, feelings, sensations, corporeal reality and psychological identity" (Ogden, 1994, p. 463) yet this individually subjective awareness can overlap in an experience of intersubjectivity. It is this overlap between the individually subjective and the intersubjective, in which "each create, negate and preserve the other" (Ogden, 1994, p. 463), that Ogden and the Relational School focus on. The analytic task, says Ogden, is not to try and separate out what belongs to whom (to attempt, in other words, to tease apart what is transference, what countertransference) but to "describe as fully as possible the specific nature of the experience of the interplay between individual subjectivity and intersubjectivity" (Ogden, 1994, p. 463), an experience Ogden calls "the analytic third". The story below describes this complicated interplay between two subjectivities in the therapeutic experience.

Using the body

Many analytic writers describe how an experience of health is synonymous with an experience of being alive in the body (Milner, 1988; Ogden, 2002) and their focus is on how therapeutic attention to physical, as well as emotional, feelings and thoughts is a vital part of facilitating this experience of aliveness.

There is often a lot of emphasis on what we think and feel during a session, but, of course, equally important is what we are experiencing in our bodies. Becoming conscious of what we ourselves are physically experiencing during a session can, as the next story illustrates, alert us to what someone is unable to verbally talk about. Similarly, becoming aware of a discrepancy between a patient's own physical expression and what she is verbally communicating can become a catalyst for significant change, especially when disassociation and disconnection from the body is a significant problem.

> I always feel vacant and sleepy in a kind of dead end way during a particular patient's session. Is this because it is early afternoon and my body wants a quick post-lunch nap, or because the patient I always see at this time overwhelms me with such a talking head barrage of babbling which I can never connect to, never find a way of being present with. I don't feel the same in the next session, and on the rare occasion when times of meeting this woman are different, I still feel switched off, so I assume it is about her more than me. So what is it about?
>
> Her very early life was full of emotional and physical upheavals. She went to six schools and lived in three countries before she was ten and had a mother whose narcissistic preoccupation with her own exciting life often took her away from her daughter emotionally as well as physically. Her father was never part of her life as he left before she was born. Is my patient's verbal bulimia a desperate attempt to get my attention in order to ward off the danger of her being emotionally abandoned again? Is my desire to switch off from her an unconscious repetition of the maternal unavailability she often experienced? Or is it an experience of the unbearable depressive emptiness that flooded her when she was so often alone and which she is terrified of returning to? By filling the space with so many empty words is she trying to shoo away the fear and terror of that early annihilating emptiness that always hovers in the wings?
>
> For a long time in the work it was all I could do to stay awake. I just couldn't find any way of engaging with what she was saying. It was all disassociated words without meaning. I would say

to her that it felt as if she was afraid of letting me have any space in the room, and that I wondered if her earlier experiences of letting someone in had resulted in such pain that she couldn't risk that again. Just as I was often temped to think about her through theory as a way of avoiding really being with her, so had she similarly retreated into a world of words without feeling, because engaging with her emotional pain was too threatening.

She was in a conflicted place of both wanting to keep me out in case I repeated her experience of abandonment, but also longing to let me in because, as coming to therapy twice a week showed, she longed and hoped for intimacy.

Months and then years went by and nothing much seemed to be shifting and I felt tired of the stuckness and began to dread these talking head sessions that pushed me to such cliff-hanging sleepy absences. I began to fantasise about getting her to use the couch so that I could nod off (and repeat her experience of maternal abandonment) without being noticed. Then, after nearly four years, I felt for the first time that something was changing. I felt more awake, and there was an occasional real sense of us being present together. For the first time since our work began, there were moments of quietness during sessions, pauses during the storm of words, a little bit of room for something else to be let in.

These changes endured and I began to tell my patient what it felt like for me, and how very glad I was to feel allowed in. Each time I said this, she would sob with a mixture of pain and relief, like a frightened, needy little girl. Her sobbing felt like the slow erosion of a block that had been holding back deep sadness and fears. The sessions started to feel like a very different place. I felt far more awake. I had managed, just, to not withdraw from her ceaseless barrage of disassociated words, and so she had managed, just, to begin to trust me as someone who could be used to feel and hear her unmet needs.

Responding to transference/countertransference experiences

How do we decide what to respond to, what to leave fallow? When is someone ready to hear what we are feeling or take back what they have projected on to us? There are no rules about when to respond to a patient's and our own unconscious communications. Timing is always a mixture of gut reaction filtered through thought. This next piece illustrates how communicating transference experiences can be greeted with a blank dismissal if the timing isn't right. The story draws on the fluidity and overlap of the various aspects of unconscious processes mentioned above: dreams, symptoms, transference processes, associations, and reveries. It describes how therapy can enable someone both to engage with what has been too painful to think about and to experience a new feeling of aliveness from becoming open to previously split-off energy.

A woman describes her life as repetitive and boring. When she gives details of an average day it is clear that she has organised her life into a series of terrifyingly rigid routines and timetables. She says she is often anxious, sometimes depressed, and says that this worsens when she has to cope with the unexpected, as it prevents her from getting through the day's task list. Somewhere along the line she has learned to be afraid of life, and has warded off this fear with timetables of control. The trouble is that these defences are now cutting her off from the very ebb and flow of the life she needs to access.

For several months I listen to the many details of her scrupulously managed life. Occasionally she is ambushed by the unexpected and this always triggers an avalanche of stress, but mostly we go round and round the same obsessive routine and I began to feel bored in a stifled kind of way. Sitting with her, and wondering how to talk about my feelings of suffocating and frustrating boredom, Freud's words ("When people grow up they cease to play") unexpectedly come to mind. It feels so very much as if this woman has forgotten how to play, and I decide to risk sharing these thoughts, but I am sharply ridiculed (as I often was during this early part of the therapy). Playing, she tells me, has a messy, infantilising ring to it and she wants none of that.

I smart a little and feel like a naughty child who has been told off for being in the way and making too much noise. Was this how she had felt during her very strict childhood: stifled, bored, frustrated, and always in the wrong? Was I feeling what she had so often experienced but had never felt able to express? These feelings persist, and despite the earlier rap on the knuckles I decide to share my thoughts. However, I am once again abruptly and severely ridiculed.

Weeks go by and sessions often feel as arid and airless as the timetabled safety she describes. Then one day she brings a dream to a session. She wasn't used to remembering her dreams and it startled her a little, this eruption from the uncontrolled depths of her being. In this dream she was sitting on the couch in the consulting room but it is somehow high up and so she is peering down at me. As she tells me the details of the strikingly omnipotent and omniscient image, it was both so ludicrous and so apposite that we each began to laugh. It was the first time I had heard her laugh, and it felt like an immense release and relief.

I often wonder why change kick-starts into action. What makes a baby begin to move down the birth canal? What makes someone suddenly open up to the more of themselves that has been too hidden in the wings? One day, or night, soon after the image of looking down on me from great heights, this woman's dream life came to her (and my) rescue. Unbidden and uncontrolled, her dreams poured forth a torrent of images that she was both overwhelmed by and intrigued with. Wild tempests filled her nights and, to start with, she struggled with them, tried to padlock the waves, attempted to build walls in the water, but to no avail.

One dream in particular made her think of a childhood holiday when she had been playing by the shoreline and had been severely told off for getting her clothes messy. Something Winnicott quotes in his brilliant book, Playing and Reality, came to mind. It was a line from the poet Tagore, and by now fairly resilient to the disparaging rebuffs delivered my way, I decided to risk sharing it: "On the seashore of endless worlds, children play". This time there was no repetition of the rebuke. This time she was (and I became) visibly moved.

Very, very slowly, little by oh so little, she made her way back to that shoreline, removed some chinks from the wall and let the sea flow in. She often told herself, and me, off for the emotional mess the process left her in. But over days, weeks, months, and years, she learned to undo habits of a lifetime and to look at both her world and herself through a different lens. The lists she used to bring to therapy of "issues to discuss" gave way to spontaneous descriptions of her inner and outer worlds: the colours of leaves in her garden, peoples faces, a piece of music, a small bird pecking in the soil, feeling the warmth of the sun on her face.

She joined an evening class and started life drawing, and was often so absorbed in her work (or was it play) that she was frequently surprised when the class ended. It was wonderful to witness the change that came over her. Like the statue of Hermione in A Winter's Tale, she was stirring back into life.

Such transformations are seldom as dramatic as hers was, and of course are never permanent or total. This woman continued to experience moods of anxiety and discontent. What was different was how she dealt with such emotions. She now often had the better of them, not them of her.

Psychotherapy can be one way amongst many of moving towards the shoreline, of nudging our familiar and often too rigidly defended worlds towards the bigger ebb and flow of unconscious processes, and discovering that not only do we not go under when we stop clinging to the familiar shape of things, but that in letting go and trusting we can actually swim.

This woman's experience clearly illustrates how an increased trust in unconscious processes enables us to change the ways we relate to our worlds. Her story made me think of Winnicott's ideas on object use (Winnicott, 1974), his belief that in order to feel deeply alive we need to be able to use our external world in a healthily, purposefully aggressive way. This woman's anticipation of having her impulsiveness rejected had made her defend herself with timetabled control, and now she was more able to use, feel, shape, and be shaped by her external world because she was less needy of a disassociated retreat for safety.

Open collaboration and open conflict

Jung once said that consciousness needs to both protect itself from and be open to the chaos of the unconscious, an emotional attitude he described as being in open conflict and open collaboration at the same time (1991b, para. 522). Because something of this capacity was present in the ways this woman now responded to intrusions from the unexpected, there was far more vitality and aliveness in her experience of living.

Her story is an exaggerated version of what many of us experience on a day to day basis. How many of us cling to timetables and routines like a child with a security blanket? How often do we take the same route to a particular destination? Stick with the same opinion of others (and ourselves) that we first settled upon months or years before? When working as therapists, how often do we cling to what we feel comfortable with rather than allow ourselves to be surprised by the unexpected?

"Experience," wrote Milner in one of her diaries, "was always bigger than the formula" (Milner, 1986b, p. 157). As the above story illustrates, learning to trust experience more than any formula is difficult to achieve and sustain and when working as a therapist, the formula/experience dialectic is a challenging one. We need to feel that we know what we are doing and that we don't know what we are doing at the same time. We need to feel secure in our knowledge of psychopathology and technique and yet feel that these are irrelevant to the experience of being with another human being. We need to be experienced by our patients as the one who knows in order to facilitate transference projections, yet we need to know that we are not the one who knows, that no one is, because there is mystery at the heart of what we do, the mystery of the unknown.

So how do we manage these paradoxes? What do we do with our pre-formulated thinking in our unformulated encounters with patients? We all know the theory about analytic reverie, intuition, empathy, and the need to focus on experience rather than explanation. But how do we manage to live this in the consulting room as well as think it outside?

The capacity of the woman above to become surprised by her inner and outer worlds and to respond to this surprise with a trust in new experience describes, it seems to me, the capacity we all need as therapists if we are to prevent these contradictions from becoming problematic. We need, in other words, to be able to give up what we thought we had to know (what Bion describes as working without memory or desire) in order to be open to what emerges between and within us. To return to Milner's words quoted at the start of this chapter, we need to be able to respond to unconscious processes with a voice that says: "Over to you."

Marion Milner's understanding of the unconscious and her belief in its essentially creative potential began long before she trained as a psychoanalyst. When she was in her twenties she began to write a diary, as she wanted to understand why she wasn't happier in her life. This diary proved to be a profoundly life-changing self-analysis, and as the following piece explores, it is a compelling reminder that we don't need the help of experts in order to reflect on our deeper, complicated life experiences.

> "My life was not as I would like it ... I was drifting without rudder or compass, swept in all directions by influence from custom, tradition, fashion ... was there no intuitive sense of how one should live, something like the instinct that prompts a dog to eat grass when he feels ill?"

So begins Marion Milner's most famous work, her first diary, A Life of One's Own. In it, through writing down her free associations, dreams, drawings, and painfully honest introspections, she learned to pay attention to the neglected parts of herself, and discovered ways of living that shifted her unhappiness. Written when she was in her twenties whilst living in London between two world wars, it is an extraordinary record of self-analysis. After completing the journal she was so astonished by the depths of what she had been able to learn about in herself that she went on to become a psychoanalyst.

Analysis can often feel very much like a reflective diary space, sometimes quite literally. I once worked with a man who wrote copious letters to me between every session, letters that he never posted and only rarely wanted to share. As a young child, he had for several years been an elective mute. Although it was a long while since he had verbally retreated from his external world and hidden behind a wall of silence, he still felt withdrawn, unable to live confidently from his own authority. Something remained unvoiced and curbed.

The letters that this man wrote were a way of breaking through some invisible wall and gathering together into one place what remained muted, neglected. It didn't matter that, although written to me, I rarely saw them. He wasn't writing or talking to me about himself. He was talking to himself about himself, both between and within sessions, because he had at last found a space where it was safe to do so.

It is not that I was redundant, that I was no part of this process. Quite the opposite, in fact. Sitting with him, I often felt like a mother whose presence is needed, somewhere in the background, for her child to get on with the serious and solitary business of play. My being there was helping him to experience what he had never known as a child: how to feel contentedly alone whilst in the presence of another.

This man was far from being alone in bringing written material to analysis. On other occasions people have shown me poems, paintings, notebooks, journals, and even actual childhood diaries. Outward expressions of the inward process of self-discovery, they are all part of the ongoing conversation that happens in therapy not just between analyst and patient, but, just as importantly, between the person seeking change and their many selves.

Ours is a culture of specialisation and expertise, and like many professions, psychoanalysis can sometimes unjustifiably cloak the ordinary in jargon-riddled language (as Oscar Wilde says about an abstruse writer in The Happy Prince: "Everyone quoted it because it was written in a language they couldn't understand"). The trouble with this obscurity is that it propagates the myth of the analyst as "the one who knows".

Too many people have an idea of psychoanalysis as a place where something is done to them, some higher knowledge imparted when they are able to receive it, and if we as therapists cannot resist trying to fulfil this expectation, people's capacity to trust their self-understanding and intuitive sense of direction can potentially be hijacked or delayed.

Marion Milner's life and work are a welcome touchstone in the maelstrom of often unnecessary psychoanalytic complication. With clarity and deep humanity, the message that shines through from all her writings is that whether with or without the help of an analyst, we each have the capacity to recover an intuitive sense of how to live rather than rely on others' frames of reference. We may choose to pay someone to help us think about things, and if we are lucky those conversations may facilitate constructive change. But at the end of the day we all have the capacity to live a life we can trust and call our own.

For Milner the process of keeping a diary enabled her to become more conscious of the gap between her conscious thoughts and the more unexpected in her life. For the man above, writing the copious letters he rarely showed helped him communicate with hidden and neglected aspects of himself. We all have our own ways of freeing ourselves up from restricted ways of thinking. Sometimes we want to share what we find in the process: Milner decided to go public and publish her diaries. Sometimes we choose to keep what we do or what we know through our dialogues with our selves hidden: the letter-writing man remained intensely private, never feeling it was safe enough to share his communications.

When is privacy pathological, when healthy? How do we know when it is helpful to "show and tell" others about our inner lives, and when it is safer to stay secret and hidden? Winnicott describes how "it is a joy to be hidden but a disaster not to be found" (Winnicott, 1963, p. 186). The next chapter explores this difficult paradox and looks at some of the ways we keep aspects of our selves hidden whilst at the same time seeking to be recognised and found.

References and suggested reading

Bion, W. (1984). *Transformations*. London: Karnac.

Evans, D. (1996). *Dictionary of Lacanian Psychoanalysis*. London and New York: Routledge.

Freud, S. (1915c). *S.E., 14*. London: Hogarth Press.

Freud, S. (1923b). Dissection of the Personality. In: *New Introductory Lectures on Psychoanalysis*, Vol. 2. Lecture 31. (Trans. James Stachey.) Harmondsworth: Penguin, 1991.

Greenson, R. R. (1972). Beyond Transference and Interpretation. *International Journal of Psycho-Analysis*, 53.

Jung, C. G. (1991a). On the Nature of the Psyche. In: *The Structures and Dynamics of the Psyche C. W. 8*. London: Routledge & Kegan Paul.

Jung, C. G. (1991b). Conscious, unconscious and individuation. In: *The Archetypes and the Collective Unconscious. C. W. 9i*. London: Routledge & Kegan Paul.

Khan, M. (1989). Beyond the dreaming experience. In: *Hidden Selves*. London: Hogarth Press.

Lacan, J. (1977). *The Four Fundamental Concepts of Psycho-Analysis*. London: Hogarth. (Reprinted London: Penguin, 1991).

Laplanche, J. & Pontalis, J. -B. (1973). *The Language of Psychoanalysis*. London: Hogarth. (Reprinted London: Karnac, 1988).

MacIntyre, A. C. (1967). *The Unconscious*. London and New York: Routledge & Kegan Paul.

Meltzer, D. (1992). *The Claustrum*. London: Karnac.

Merleau-Ponty, M. (2002). *Phenomenology of Perception*. Oxon and New York: Routledge & Kegan Paul.

Milner, M. (1986). *An Experiment in Leisure*. London: Virago.

Milner, M. (1986b). *A Life of One's Own*. London: Virago.

Milner, M. (1987). *Eternity's Sunrise*. London: Virago.

Milner, M. (1987b). Afterthoughts. In: *The Suppressed Madness of Sane Men*. London, New York: Routledge.

O'Connor, N. (2010). *Questioning Identities; Philosophy in Psychoanalytic Practice*. London: Karnac.

Ogden, T. H. (1994). The analytic third. In: S. A. Mitchell & L. Aron (Eds.), *Relational Psychoanalysis: the Emergence of a Tradition*. London: Analytic Press, 1999.

Ogden, T. H. (2002). *Conversations at the Frontier of Dreaming*. London: Karnac.

Peters, R. (1991). The therapist's expectation of the transference. *Journal of Analytical Psychology, 36*.

Phillips, A. (1995). Dreams. In: *Terrors and Experts*. London: Faber and Faber.

Szasz, T. (1963). The concept of transference. *International Journal of Psycho-Analysis, 44*.

Winnicott, D. W. (1963). Communicating and not communicating leading to a study of certain opposites. In: *The Maturational Process and the Facilitating Environment*. London: Hogarth Press, 1990.

Winnicott, D. W. (1974). The use of an object and relating through identifications. In: *Playing and Reality*. London: Penguin.

Zia, P. (1994). Extract from unpublished notebooks.

CHAPTER THREE

Secrets and silences

Who can say whether in essence fire is destructive or constructive?

—Donald Winnicott

As the last chapter explored, a lot of what happens in therapy involves freeing us up to reflect on what we have often spent years managing not to address. It is a process that invariably triggers a complicated mixture of fears and freedom. Becoming more aware of our unconscious life can be hugely empowering: the woman with the "fish out of water" dream in the last chapter, for example, discovered that understanding what her desperate hunger was connected with enabled her to bear conflicts better, and her relationship with both herself and others flourished as a result.

Hers was an almost fairy tale story of transformation, but the process of emotional change can often increase anxiety stakes. The very denials and defences that are restricting us are also the comfortingly familiar habits of a lifetime and there is usually a tug of war between loss and gain. How can we be sure that what is being uncovered or discovered during therapy is going to lead to a good thing? What if change unsteadies us from knowing what we want and who we are? What if we do not like what we find? What if others do not love us any more when we bring aspects of ourselves out of hiding? As a patient once said to me: "I'm discovering that therapy can make you less nice."

As awareness develops about our desire for, yet fear of, change, there is often an uncomfortable waiting-room kind of time when familiar ways of responding are no longer working very well but new ways are still on shaky ground. Therapy can be a space where we can let ourselves feel open to the discomfort of doubt, and different ways of reflecting and communicating can be tested out. Sometimes these are talked about, sometimes they remain private. As a patient said to me recently: "I don't want you to think that this is all of me, I mean what I am telling you now isn't everything; there are other things I haven't said, things I can't."

As touched on at the end of the last chapter, our challenge as therapists is to know whether to encourage communication or to respect the need for silence. As Khan says: "The question is whether privacy constitutes a relatedness to the True Self or a paranoid and aggressive exclusion of others from any link with it" (Khan, 1969). If we intrude too much or too soon we risk deepening a patient's need to stay hidden because of an earlier experience of impingement. If we never challenge what Winnicott calls "the right not to communicate" we may fail to facilitate True Self expression (Winnicott, 1963).

As changes occur in this private/shared dynamic, so does the way the therapeutic relationship is experienced. The following story is an illustration of this multilayered hide and seek process.

Learning to be Hidden

> Early in our work together a woman tells me about a dream that has been dogging her for years. It takes different forms but the central motif is the same. She is rooted to the spot and unable to speak. Sometimes she's on stage, sometimes with friends; often in front of a class (in her working life she is a teacher). In some dreams she is a child, in others an adult. Always there is a paralysing feeling of being unable to make her voice heard and being unable to move.
>
> Jung once said that the first dreams brought to therapy often chart the course and meaning of analytic work. In that sense, the beginning anticipates the ending. This was certainly true for this woman. Over the next seven years our work was, in a way,

all about making sense of this muted image, and challenging it. It spilled into her daily life in the form of inhibition, social anxiety (this being the overt cause for her coming to see a therapist), and being far too much the echo of others' demands and opinions. At its root was a deep fear of aggressive rejection if she expressed herself to another.

As a child my patient's father was both physically and emotionally violent, and she had experienced him as frighteningly dominating and aggressively unable to tolerate any differences of opinion. Her mother had chosen acquiescence as the safest way to negotiate his sadistic bullying, and my patient had unthinkingly followed suit. Only now, in her early thirties, was she painfully discovering that being muted to feel safe didn't really work.

From the start of our work together, this fear of self-expression was transferred on to our relationship. Well into the first year, I was often struck by the feeling of her absence more than presence. It was as if she was afraid to leave her imprint in the room. Always wanting me to lead the way, she was most comfortable being the hesitant and responding echo. Recognising the clear connection between my experience of her as absent and her lack of voice in the dreams bothered her. Hiding had been safe. But the prospect of a lifetime of frozen compliance made her determined to shift this pattern, and something in her kick-started a desire to fight back.

For a long while her struggle remained internal. I often felt frustrated and irritated by her limpet-like passivity and a couple of times a fantasy of wanting to angrily shake her put me in touch not only with what she had experienced from her father but the hidden aggression she felt towards herself, me, and the wider world around her.

For what at times felt like an eternity, sessions were full of lengthy silences. As therapists we tend to focus on how therapy is a talking cure, but of course there is also the parallel need to let people keep things hidden; the need to respect, as Winnicott puts it, the right not to communicate. This woman reminded me of that need in a way that sometimes felt unbearable. For a long while her silences felt like a regressive repetition of the old stuck groove but at some point in the work I realised the quietness felt different. There was a visceral sense of her struggling to break into something healthier.

It can be comforting to have verbal exchanges to keep us in the loop of what is going on, but perhaps the most profound changes of all need to happen out of our talking reach, in silence.

At some point in the work, there was another clear shift. Like a teenager who just can't be arsed, she started to turn up late and express boredom with therapy in an irritable manner. We talked a lot about how finding a voice felt somewhat developmental: she had never had the adolescent experience of defining herself against the other. There had only ever been anxious compliance and emotional retreat. With this bolshie, and sometimes sullen, teenager in the room with me, at last and at least we could talk and even joke about it, and things were somehow on the move.

The surly teenage phase did its bit, and in time, over time, I began to realise there was this young woman in the room with me who was trusting and finding her own voice. During the first stage of therapy she had always felt like either a very young child or quite an old person, then there had been the teenage phase, and now it felt as if she had become closer to her chronological mid-thirties.

These shifts began to be played out in her relationships with others. It didn't come easily, but she fought hook, line, and sinker to resist the habit of retreat in the face of emotional encounter. Sessions would often involve a painstaking scrutiny of conversations that had happened or were going to happen with friends or colleagues in order to imagine how she could feel more present, and she would agonise over whether her voice had really been heard. Emotional retreat often remained an instinctive get out clause, and maybe to some degree it always would, but a genuine hunger for intimacy was developing in her. When therapy ended, there was a real sense of her being more present than absent, and so a feeling that far less of her was in hiding, far more available to be found.

Winnicott: True and False Self

In "Ego distortion in terms of True and False Self" (1960) Winnicott explores our need for what he calls True and False Selves. In his view, the True Self reveals itself early on in life through spontaneous play.

If our early imaginative gestures are welcomed and given root room, then our experiences of true self can develop and flourish. We will then carry within us a capacity for aliveness essential for our mental health. At some stage in development, argues Winnicott, we need to develop a False Self in order to fit in with the myriad of compromises and conformities that are part and parcel of any family and wider social life, but ideally we grow up with a conscious and working partnership between the two: accommodating our need to fit in with the world around us with our equally strong need to experience authenticity and spontaneity.

Many people, like the woman above, suffer deeply from having had their True Self gestures repeatedly rejected. The result is often an overidentification with the False Self (which Jung would call the persona), a fitting in to external demands in order to feel secure. When this imbalance occurs, people frequently describe feeling empty and unheard. Like the woman above, they feel as if they have lost their own voice, and also like her there is the tendency to keep intimacy at arm's length. Too readily compliant and too unable to trust their own instinctive responses, intimacy feels like a threatening impingement that the self needs to be protected from. As one patient said: "How can I have relationships with people when I don't feel real myself."

The therapeutic challenge when working with someone who is experiencing this feeling of not being real is to ensure they do not feel pressured to communicate. As noted above in relation to the Khan quote and explored through stories in Chapter One, an experience of this kind of pressure may either encourage a patient to bring material to the session that they think might interest or impress, or trigger an even deeper retreat because of feeling impinged upon.

The story of the woman above ends on a positive note, but of course not everyone who comes to therapy manages to communicate True Self experience in a constructively shared way. Many people feel such anxiety about upsetting the status quo within and without that the restricting safety of the familiar is preferable to the terror of opening floodgates on to the unknown. The next piece is about how the regressive pull of fantasy enables people to stay in retreat when the challenge of engagement and intimacy feels too frightening to manage. I've drawn upon Winnicott's distinction between fantasying and dreaming (Winnicott, 1974) as I find it a useful way of distinguishing between destructive and constructive uses of imagination.

Dreaming, fantasying, and living

The young woman opposite me talks in a tone of dreamy vagueness. Listening to her, I am lulled into a world of fantasy, a world peppered with daydreams of what might be or could have been. She describes the novel she might one day write, the travelling she may one day embark on, the colleague she has a crush on but who remains unaware of the fictional romance being woven around her. Although all of her imaginings have some connection to events in the outside world, the thread is mostly very distant and tenuous. And yet the animation with which she describes her various worlds of make-believe at times almost persuades me that she is talking about the real. After listening to her for some time I begin to feel a little uncomfortable. It is as if I am travelling with her in some air balloon, gazing with pleasure at the landscape below, yet utterly failing to establish any foothold on the reality of that terrain.

I find myself thinking of another patient I saw several years previously who always brought a notebook to sessions full of dreams, sketches, and poetry. During session after session he would read from notebooks, often bringing his latest dreams. I usually enjoy working with dreams: they can have a valuable and subversive knack of saying it as it is. Yet it had seemed to me that he was using this notebook as a way of hiding from himself and others.

The daydreaming of both these people had an asexual quality to it because in different ways they were both afraid of experiencing their own desires. For other people, masturbatory sexual fantasy is used to avoid connecting sexual hunger with hunger for loving intimacy. "Women are such a disappointment," a man in early middle age tells me. "They may look good, but as soon as things begin to take off, their emotional neediness gets in the way. Why can't sex with a woman be like porn?" He knows, he tells me a little shamefacedly, that it's not good to use porn too much, but it's difficult to resist when it's so much easier to get what he wants from virtual reality than from real flesh and blood. His comments reflect an increasingly large number of people, predominantly men, who are not in any nurturing relationships and are addicted to porn because the arousal it offers is instant, and the emotional capacity needed to experience a mutually loving and sexually fulfilling relationship is too frightening a challenge.

In his paper "Dreaming, fantasying and living" Winnicott makes the distinction between regressive fantasy that is disassociated from the lived life of the individual and the use of fantasy to re-imagine our external world in a way that positively transforms. It is a vital distinction in therapeutic work, which is so much about the kindling of dreams and imagination.

The examples above illustrate the use of fantasy to avoid engaging with the actualities of the world. For each of these people, immersion in their dreaming lives enabled them to exclude others from their hidden selves. Both of the men described above found it immensely difficult to feel at ease with themselves when with others, as they always experienced intimacy as demanding and intrusive. They compensated for this by withdrawing to the safer intensity of porn or dreams. Both obsessions provided an instant kind of gratification and protection from what they were afraid of looking at, but because the escape route was so disassociated from genuine aliveness it failed to lead anywhere constructive.

The young woman above was also using her daydreams to avoid facing up to her fear of her hunger for life. She didn't know how to find what she wanted from others and the daydreams were her way of assuaging the ache of that unmet need. However, unlike the two men described above, she expressed a longing to find a way of engaging less fearfully and more deeply with life. She reminded me of *Amélie*, the film about a young woman whose delightful capacity for fantasy enables her, for a while at least, to avoid facing the reality of her own unlived life.

Retreating from the terror of remembered pain

There are many ways of hiding from ourselves and others. Some of them have names. Anorexia, autism, obsessive, compulsive, and phobic behaviours can, like fantasying, be ways of avoiding engaging with others because of underlying terrors and anxieties about becoming smothered and engulfed. The next story is about how letting behaviour become controlled by a tyranny of thoughts can offer the illusion of safety from such anxieties.

A neatly dressed woman suddenly yawns several times, and tells me she is tired as she has been up since 5am. She often gets up early because otherwise there is not time to do the things that need to be done. No day has enough time in it for her to do the things she needs to do, so she often works into the night in order to feel she is on top of it all.

She works as the secretary to a successful businessman, and knows she is more efficient than most of her colleagues, but the more she does the more work her boss keeps giving her and as she is a perfectionist who does not know how to say no this often eats into her evenings and weekends.

The trouble is, she tells me, that this means there is not enough time for keeping her home in order. She is worried because this has become quite an obsessive preoccupation. She cannot make herself stop once she starts cleaning, because some part of her will not let up until the whole flat is spotless. And she is concerned about what this is doing to her. Something happened the other week, she tells me, that made her really worried.

She tells me that she had invited some friends for Sunday lunch with their two children. She had not seen them for a while, and had spent a lot of time getting the place ready and thinking of food that two and four year-olds might eat. She had been looking forward to the event, but what actually happened was simple and terrible chaos. The children had run riot around her home. The two-year-old had peed on her rug. She had hated every minute and wanted them to leave so that she could put everything back in order.

After they eventually left and she was clearing up, she had a sudden flashback to her own childhood. Her mother, like her, used to clean the house obsessively and she suddenly recalled coming back from school one day with a friend and wanting to play in her bedroom. Her mother had shouted at her that they had to play outside because the floor had just been cleaned and the carpet hoovered. She remembered how embarrassed she had felt, and how her friend had turned away and said that she wanted to go to her own home. "And now," she says, "I have become like my mother. Unable to let life in because a clean house has become more important than human relationships."

All of us have ways of trying to impose some kind of order upon our internal and external worlds. Many people use lists. Many work at weekends. But for some people, like the woman above, continually striving for control has developed into a pattern of behaviour over which she has no control. Although able to see how punitive, exhausting, and lonely it is to collude with the part of her that demands perfection, she is utterly terrified of loosening the hold this tyranny has over her.

So why can't this woman take her foot off the pedal? Why can't she stop hiding behind tyrannical routines of cleanliness? Why is the experience of unkempt life so terrifying? As she herself said, at one level she has learned to be like her mother. As a teenager, her mother had experienced a major psychotic breakdown. My patient was unsure of the details but it had required hospitalisation and induced much fear and shame. Then during her early twenties, this woman had herself suffered a breakdown. Unlike her mother she hadn't been hospitalised, but the terror of the experience and fear of it returning was strong. Winnicott's observation that the breakdown we are afraid of having is the breakdown that has already happened is apposite here. During her own childhood this woman had learned to unconsciously identify with her mother's ways of trying to ward off any return of illness. Her exhausting and lonely need to create order over chaos made her at some level feel safe.

Working with such a strongly entrenched resistance to change can be profoundly challenging and disturbing. When defences are a protection against memory of a psychotic or severe breakdown there's a need to tread gently because of the knowledge that fire can be more destructive than constructive. This woman's fear of being overwhelmed by the turmoil of inner chaos meant that therapy needed to help her understand and manage rather than dismantle defences, so that her world wasn't flooded with the uncontrollable terror of breakdown.

Life is elsewhere

For some people, the experience of feeling deeply alive is created through moments of intensity that are sought away from the everyday and familiar. They seek out emotional "highs" through behaviour that is often kept separate from their "normal" lives because they have never experienced the aliveness they are hungry for within the framework of the "normal". Sometimes described as the Peter Pan syndrome, their behaviour is fuelled by always feeling more restless than restful on home ground.

The man I am sitting with is in his late thirties, but if I didn't know this it would be hard to guess his age. He has, as always, come to the session straight from jogging, and his running shoes, T-shirt, and track suit add to an impression of boyish, almost androgynous, youthfulness. We have worked together for several years, and over that time one image in particular has come to encapsulate the anguish he repeatedly finds himself in. Drawn from a dream he had early on, it is the image of a bird in flight, soaring and circling high above the world. He easily identifies with this bird. When in flight (and with a passion for mountaineering he almost literally often is) he feels on top of his world. During these times he feels the same as he does whenever he falls in love: wonderfully alive, inspired and inspiring. But when the flight ends, whether because the mountain climb is over or some love affair has past its peak, there is a terrible spiralling down to an abyss of bleak despair.

This pattern of flight and fall has been described by analytic theory in different ways: Balint's description of the philobat in Thrills and Regressions is of someone who often prefers to be on their own and enjoys activities that can make them fly high (Balint coined the term philobat from acrobat, someone who seeks intensity away from the safety of the earth). Meltzer talks about those who experience the fall from the hubris of grandiosity to the horror of claustrophobia, whilst for Jung this pattern of flight and fall is embedded in the notion of the puer aeternus: the eternal youth who retains an adolescent horror of growing up. First coined by Ovid in his description of Icarus, the Greek god who flew too close to the sun and so fell to his death in the sea below, the puer aeternus is probably best known in our Western culture through Peter Pan, J. M. Barrie's spirited creation whose flight from becoming adult took him to Neverland.

Psychological interpretations of this kind of behaviour tend to focus upon what is being escaped from. Women and men who easily get bored by routine and who lack a certain staying power necessary for tethering themselves down to the world, are, it is argued, essentially escaping from a difficult early relationship with their respective fathers and mothers. To clip their wings would mean feeling smothered by the alienating world around them. Survival depends upon escaping any nets of False Self commitment and searching instead for further flights into moments of intensity.

Many who identify with this way of living satisfy their hunger for fiery passion by becoming Don Juan figures. Others feed their need for a "high" through extreme sports: the vertiginous film Man on Wire about Phillipe Petit's addiction to literally flying high is a powerful portrait of this. Others find their highs through drugs: the so called "Forever 27 club" that now has Amy Winehouse's name added to it is full of those who, like Icarus, flew too close to the sun.

Sometimes an early trigger that explains this need for flight is clear. At other times there is simply and deeply a forlorn feeling of emotional homelessness from the whole package of early family and later life The man above, for example, suffered much emotional pain in his early years because of a lengthy and acrimonious parental divorce. He had never known the feeling of being comfortably on home ground because his experience of relationships was dominated by what was false and barbed. From an early age he developed the capacity to take refuge from unhappiness by seeking out moments of intensity, both physical and emotional. These flights from his world gave him a tremendous feeling of freedom from all that had sapped and trapped him in life. But they were essentially transient. There was always the descent. And he always had difficulty in finding his feet in the mundane routines of the everyday.

There is much value in what Peter Pans bring to our world. Like the archetypal adolescent, they are full of youthful energy and intensity and have the capacity to challenge and transform the staid and fixed. But like Peter Pan, and the man above, there is often a poignant sense of emotional homelessness about such people, a feeling that unless they can learn to graft some of their energy to the routine of the everyday, home is always elsewhere as they restlessly search for a moment of further intensity.

A poem by Yeats entitled "An Irish Airman Forsees His Death" encapsulates for me how the emotional intensity experienced in the Neverland of flight can become tragically more important than the felt limitations of everyday life:

> A lonely impulse of delight
> Drove to this tumult in the clouds:
> I balanced all, brought all to mind,

> The years to come seemed waste of breath,
> A waste of breath the years behind
> In balance with this life, this death.

Struggling with being found

People often begin therapy when some secret behaviour has been found out and found unacceptable. The drugs, infidelities, thefts, or gambling have been seen from outside in rather than from the inside out and judged as destructive and immoral. Often there is conflict between a subjective experience of behaviour as positive and enabling and guilt-ridden identification with wider family and social reactions.

It is assumed that as therapists our role is to listen to someone's subjective experience respectfully and non-judgementally, yet is it possible to leave our personal ideas about what constitutes emotional health out of the therapeutic relationship? To paraphrase Bion again, can we really work without imposing any memory of, or desire for, our particular brand of living on to the patient when behaviour is self-destructive or destructive to others and clashes problematically with social and cultural moralities we may identify with?

As my clinical reflections illustrate, although behaviour may be perceived as socially deviant it is often unconsciously chosen as a conflicted and turbulent way of staying emotionally alive. Because of this there can be a strong sense of the purposeful and dynamic, as well as the negative and guilty, in someone's experience of potentially destructive behaviour. Within the complexity of this intense conflict there is often a sense of intentional sincerity developing. By sincerity I am thinking of Khan's reference to it as "a congruence between avowal and actual feeling" (Khan, 1989, p. 12). Often in therapy there is an almost palpable intention of someone struggling to find a way of linking what is too destructively hidden with what needs to be more recognised and found.

There is a wonderful soliloquy by Prince Hal in *Henry IV* which expresses this subjective fluidity. At this stage in the play Hal is the troublesome Peter Pan of the royal household, as despite being heir to the throne he hangs out with hard core drinkers, bullies, scroungers, thieves, and prostitutes. Probably pushed in this direction by a mixture of boredom, unresolved difficulties with his father, and the impossible pressure to be an A-star soldier, Hal is perceived by his family and friends as a delinquent, and largely treated as a write-off. His soliloquy describes the changes evolving within him that the outside world is unaware of: his intention to show a different side of himself, a Hal that can link authentic self-expression to a sincere experience of public persona and so break the either/or of the True/False self deadlock.

> So, when this loose behaviour I throw off
> And pay the debt I never promisèd,
> By how much better than my word I am,
> By so much shall I falsify men's hopes;
> And like bright metal on a sullen ground,
> My reformation, glitt'ring o'er my fault,
> Shall show more goodly and attract more eyes
> Than that which hath no foil to set it off.
> I'll so offend to make offence a skill,
> Redeeming time when men think least I will.

> (Henry 1V Part 1: Act 1 Sc. 2)

Hal's soliloquy describes the kind of inner monologue that, as therapists, we often have the privilege of being entrusted with. Below is a story about a woman for whom, like Hal, parental approval was painfully scant. Her emotional neglect often triggered socially unacceptable acting out but as she (again like Hal) found out, this only increased criticism and rejection. For years she seesawed between identifying with her mother's view on things in order to feel accepted and reacting against this unhealthy collusion with an attempt to find and meet her own needs. Even after her mother's death this tug of war behaviour was still determining her life. She came to therapy to try and free herself from the compulsion to repeat.

Early in our work together a woman in her mid-thirties is distressed by the following dream. More of a nightmare than a dream, it unleashes torrents of grief which she is unable to contain. The dream is very short, and at one level very simple. In it, an eighteen-year-old girl walks towards her. She is lost and crying.

My patient awoke from the dream with tears streaming down her face. Almost exactly eighteen years before the dream she had had an abortion. The further painful twist to this tale was that she herself had been eighteen at the time. So what was the dream about? Bereavement for the child she had never known? Or for the young woman she had been who had become so lost?

My patient was, she tells me, always a difficult child. She had a brother who was the apple of her mother's eye. Her father had died when she was only five from an asthma attack, and she remembers the terrible change that came over her mother. She became frightened of her coldness and strictness. "She adored my brother. Partly I guess because he looked so much like Dad. But me and Mum just never got on."

In her early teens my patient discovered the power of her sexuality. She was extraordinarily pretty, and was soon using her capacity to make heads turn for her own comfort. From an early age she had many casual sexual relationships. It never crossed her mind that sex was about trying to find the succour and intimacy she had never had from her mother.

Her mother got to hear about her daughter's behaviour and threatened to throw her out of home. Their relationship continued to deteriorate, with maternal rejection exacerbating her sexual acting out. And then one day she discovered she was pregnant. She had no idea who the father was, and decided to have an abortion. "I remember thinking: I must get rid of it because Mum will kill me if she finds out."

Shortly after the abortion, her promiscuous defence broke down and she went utterly to pieces. Like the girl in the dream, she was eighteen years old, lost and crying. One day, broken with distress and shame she returned home to ask for her mother's forgiveness. It came gradually but at a cost. And the cost was compliance. In return for maternal acceptance she became an echo of her mother's way of seeing. Frigidity replaced promiscuity and self-blame crushed the libidinous acting out. After defying her mother for so many years, she now colluded with the maternal view of her younger self as wicked and shameless. "For years my mother and I dressed the same, ate the same food, we were the same." It was her mother's death that prompted her to start therapy, and the long process of disidentifying from her mother's way of seeing things began.

Something of this woman's experience of authenticity was part of her teenage sexual behaviour: sex gave her a good feed, a sense of being held, and emotional intensity that she hungered for and had never had sufficient of from her mother. So she was doing something that made her feel alive but that was judged by the world around her as bad. For her the fire had been at some level constructive but for her mother it was destructive. And in needing her mother's approval, she adhesively identified with her damning judgement.

Destructive or constructive?

Her breakdown happened before she started therapy, but often it is when analytic work is really getting under way and restricting self-identifications are breaking down that people start to act out in ways that are usually thought of as delinquent and potentially dangerous: drugs, promiscuity, and stealing are the most frequent behaviours that come to mind.

As mentioned above, this development can feel hugely challenging. A year or so into their different therapies and one woman I am working with becomes a sex worker, while a man takes up gambling and appears to be in real danger of losing his livelihood.

How can we trust that these kinds of behaviours are part of a bigger process of someone struggling to develop a healthier sense of self? How can we not trust this? If we panic and stick our censorious oar in, whether consciously or unconsciously, surely we are in danger of putting ourselves on the same page as the judgemental mother in the story above.

Only in retrospect could I really understand that the behaviour of both the man and woman mentioned above had been ways of releasing and working through earlier restrictions and traumas. Below is a fuller description of the woman's story to illustrate this process more clearly.

> During her late teens this woman had been sexually abused by her father. Having left home shortly after she was born and emigrated to another country, he returned unexpectedly at a time in her life when she was extremely emotionally vulnerable. Her relationship with her depressed mother had always been difficult and from her early teenage years, sex, booze, and drugs were often used as ways of finding some kind of intensity and attention. Her relationship with her stranger-father soon became sexualised and she felt

adored in the way she craved. One day her mother found out about the incestuous relationship and this woman quickly colluded with the shame and disgust that was being expressed and felt full of self-blame.

During therapy she was able for the first time to acknowledge the ambivalence of her feelings about what had happened. The sexual contact with her known but unknown father had been emotionally gratifying as well as shameful because it had made her feel deeply alive and loved.

Shortly after acknowledging, by re-experiencing, this ambivalence she started to work as a sex worker. It seemed that having intense, unattached sex with usually older men was a way of gratifying the physical and emotional hunger that therapy had enabled her to recognise. The sex work continued for about fifteen months, and during this time I was often concerned about her safety. Then she quite unexpectedly stopped this work, in a sense weaned herself from it, and soon after began her first "proper" relationship with a man which proved to be genuine and loving. It felt as if she had allowed her hidden needs to be spilled out not just in therapy but also on to the outside world, pursuing the only way she knew to feel nourished. And that this process had been more restorative than regressive or destructive.

People who live on the potentially destructive edge of things often surprisingly manage, as she did, to regress in order to find a healthier way of managing emotional pain and complexity. Sometimes the emotional damage seems too severe and deep for this kind of reparation to be possible. But the inherently purposeful nature of psyche means that there is often constructive intention in the actions people feel compelled to take. Often we may not be able to see or understand that there is some kind of unconscious method in what may look like destructive madness, but we have to try and trust. Milner describes this process in *The Hands of the Living God*:

> Some patients seem to be aware ... of a force in them to do with growth, growth towards their own shape ... something that seemed to be sensed as driving them to break down false inner organisations which do not really belong to them; something which can also be deeply feared as a kind of creative fury ... also feared because

of the temporary chaos it must cause when the integrations on a false basis are being broken down in order that a better one may emerge.

(Milner, 1988, pp. 384–385)

The next story is about how a patient's compulsion to steal, which developed after therapy began, ended up being understood as not only about her own emotional deprivation but also her unconscious response to her husband's hidden behaviour.

After working together for several months a woman tells me that she has started compulsively stealing expensive items of clothing. She never wears these items, but hoards them away under the marital bed. Occasionally, when feeling lonely, she roots out and fingers some material. She is terrified of being caught but can't stop herself from doing it.

It is not her first story of theft. Early on in our sessions she told me of an incident that happened when she was about six years old. With a similar compulsive drive, she had for many months stolen marbles from a local toy shop. Very occasionally she would take one or two to school but the bulk of the hoard remained hidden under her mattress. Like the current clothing stash, she would now and again get secret pleasure from fingering the glass beads.

When trying to understand what had triggered these marble thefts, I had asked her what had been happening in her life when she was six. She said that her elder sister, whom she both envied and adored, had at this time been very poorly and in hospital for many months and she had often had to stay with a relative who she didn't like and where she had felt homesick. Parental preoccupation with her ill sibling and the feeling of being abandoned, both physically and emotionally, had obviously had a traumatic effect. It became possible to understand the stealing as a way of taking something back from the environment during this time of emotional neglect. Certainly, this early bout of stealing stopped at the same time as her sisters homecoming, and so the return of more consistent parental love.

But what of her more recent thefts and hiding? Why this return to an earlier pattern of acting out? Was it because therapy was putting her in touch with feelings of emotional abandonment she had suffered long ago? Certainly in the transference there was the strong felt, but mostly unspoken, needy anger that I could never give her enough. She always arrived early for sessions, and always found breaks very difficult to cope with.

My patient's marriage had been the overt reason for her initially requesting therapy. She was deeply confused, because although she felt very loving towards her husband, he just seemed to be emotionally elsewhere. She was often needy of reassurance in the relationship: he was a good deal older than her and she often felt more like an anxious, clinging child than a strong woman.

One day she arrived for a session looking exhausted but somehow unburdened. She had discovered that her husband had been having an affair for almost a year. He had broken down and confessed after she by chance found a love letter in his pocket. She felt sad, terribly sad, but the desire to (like her husband) secretly take what wasn't hers ended almost overnight.

Amongst both children and adults, stealing is very common. For children, theft is most usually of money, food, and sweets, both within and outside of the home. Theorists such as Winnicott and Bowlby have repeatedly connected such childhood thefts with emotional deprivation. Children who, like my patient above, suddenly feel the loss of a loving environment are especially prone to stealing: acting out the pain of loss by greedily taking and often hoarding whatever brings excitement and succour.

For adults, theft becomes a far more complicated issue, as there are many ways of stealing in order to fill some needy gap. Adults, like children, often take what isn't rightfully theirs when feeling insecure, neglected, unloved. Often, as with children, the theft is of food, clothing, or money. Yet also in adult behaviour there are less obvious thefts used to ward off emptiness. The "stolen moments" of love affairs, for example, can be used as a way of warding off deep-seated feelings of emptiness.

The husband of my patient was, it turned out, very much using his affair to feed a hunger that the marriage hadn't been able to reach. He had been unhappy in the marriage for some time. Their sex life had become virtually non-existent and he increasingly felt more like a father figure than a husband in the relationship. But he had been terrified of telling his wife how he felt as he was afraid that her emotional vulnerability meant that she wouldn't be able to cope.

The discovery of their very different kinds of thefts enabled them to start to understand the underlying issues. They worked with a therapist who helped them understand that their way of relating was preventing them from growing, either separately or together. They decided, after much anguish, to separate, and I continued to work with the woman. For the first time in her adult life she stopped depending on either another person or an illegal action to make herself feel alive, and began to discover and trust her own much neglected potential.

This chapter has focussed on some of the ways we try to hide aspects of our emotional complexity from each other and from ourselves, often only showing what matches the person we think of ourselves as being and hiding or repressing what is too painful to be seen. For most people, what is concealed and what revealed is never fixed, because different relationships enable different aspects of who we are becoming to emerge. As one woman said to me after several years of therapy: "When I first started therapy I didn't even know so much of me was hidden. Nowadays I can feel that hidden part of me. It's familiar. I like it. But I don't always feel safe showing it to others. Sometimes I do, but sometimes I need to keep it under wraps."

As the last story clearly illustrates, however hidden or under wraps we may think we are being, there is no such thing as a separate self. As Winnicott succinctly puts it: "There is no such thing as a baby" (Winnicott, 1964, p. 88), meaning that none of our subjective experiences are separate from the influence of relationship. The impact of both immediate family and wider socio-political culture plays a significant part in how we are continually discovering ourselves to be.

Was, for example, the woman who stole marbles as a child unconsciously transferring an expectation of her earlier abandonment on to her marital relationship? Was her asexual and childlike manner a response to her husband's absence, or because of the way she had learned to express herself as a woman? Did he start an affair because she was sexually unavailable, or because he was unable to be deeply sexual and deeply loving at the same time?

The next chapter focuses on the complexity of our experiences of relationship and why it is so often difficult to know when a relationship is a relationship with another separate person and not just a conversation with our selves.

References and suggested reading

Balint, M. (1987). *Thrills & Regressions*. London: Karnac.

Chopin, K. (2003). *The Awakening*. London: Penguin. (A short novel that beautifully and painfully captures the emotional struggle to find a way of making what has been hidden lived and so found.)

Eigen, M. (1993). *The Electrified Tightrope* (Ed. Phillips, A.). Pennsylvania: Aronson.

Khan, M. (1969). Vicissitudes of being, knowing and experiencing in the therapeutic situation. *British Journal of Medical Psychology, 42:* 383–393.

Khan, M. (1974). *The Privacy of the Self.* London: Hogarth Press.

Khan, M. (1989). *Hidden Selves.* London: Karnac.

Milner, M. (1988). *The Hands of the Living God.* London: Virago Press.

Pines, D. (2010). *A Woman's Unconscious Use of Her Body.* Sussex and New York: Routledge.

Tustin, F. (1986). *Autistic Barriers in Neurotic Patients.* London: Karnac.

Winnicott, D. W. (1960). Ego distortion in terms of True and False Self. In: *The Maturational Process and the Facilitating Environment.* London: Hogarth Press, 1990.

Winnicott, D. W. (1963). Communicating and not communicating leading to a study of certain opposites. In: *The Maturational Process and the Facilitating Environment.* London: Hogarth Press, 1990.

Winnicott, D. W. (1964). *The Child, the Family and the Outside World.* London: Penguin.

Winnicott, D. W. (1974). Dreaming, fantasying and living. In: *Playing and Reality.* London: Penguin.

Yeoman, A. (1998). *Now or Neverland: Peter Pan and the Myth of Eternal Youth.* Toronto: Inner City Books.

CHAPTER FOUR

In search of others

There is no such thing as a baby

—Donald Winnicott

As the stories so far illustrate, however separate we may feel, and try to be, from each other, we are all deeply impacted by relationship. This chapter is about the centrality of this fact in our emotional lives. Winnicott's dictum that there is no such thing as a baby (meaning that a baby's experience of her existence is inseparable from her maternal relationship) was a departure from Freud's view that there *was* such a thing as a baby. For Freud, we start life with autoerotic rather than relational drives, so the infant reaches for a feed because of self-centred impulses rather than hunger for intimacy.

Most contemporary therapists work from the premise that from the beginning of life we are in a state of intense relatedness. How we were held, fed, gazed at, and loved as infants will significantly influence how secure or anxious we feel in relation to both ourselves and others and determine whether we are able to experience others as different from, as well as similar to, ourselves. Individual theorists have approached this premise from particular perspectives, and some of these perspectives have become the focus of specific psychoanalytic groups: Object Relations, The Middle Group, Attachment Theory, Lacanian, and The Relational School are some of these.

There are many books that clearly explain the differences between these various perspectives (Klein, 1987; Waddell, 1998) and my concern here is not with the specifics of that continuing story, but two strikingly different ways of understanding our earliest experiences of relationship are worth mentioning.

The first is the object relations focus on the (m)other-infant dyad compared to the wider attention given to socio-political and cultural influences and intersubjective perspectives by writers such as Benjamin and Orbach within the phenomenological and Relational School (Benjamin, 1990). How much we understand an individual's development of self-identity as emerging from influences beyond the immediate environment is something both this chapter and the next explores.

The second variance exists in how the impact of the infant's experience of mirroring is interpreted. For Winnicott (Winnicott, 1974) a good enough experience of feeling mirrored by the mother's loving gaze facilitates an experience of authentic subjectivity and enables a healthy capacity to tolerate separateness to begin. Whereas for Lacan (Lacan, 1977), identifying with the reflected image of ourselves during the "mirror stage" creates a narcissistic illusion of completeness, and any subsequent emotional growth involves the pain of recognising the lack or insufficiency within this internalised image.

Whatever our particular theoretical focus, therapy is about how a person's experience of relationships (intra and interpsychically) is communicated through the therapeutic relationship so that what has become inappropriately and repetitively defended can be renegotiated and changed. As the following case examples show, this understanding occurs on different levels; there is attention to unconscious processes in the "here and now" of the therapeutic relationship, a gathering of memories about a patient's past, absorption of the daily happenings and preoccupations that have occurred between sessions, and a trust in the purposefulness of what is taking shape.

Experiencing more anxiety than containment in our early environment makes our growth towards separation fraught with fears, and for many people a secure sense of where they end and where the other begins has never developed. As Freud said, we all suffer from a compulsion to repeat, and angers and terrors that were never recognised or held during infancy are often still rampaging about in adult life. As well as engaging with these feelings through unconscious processes, a patient's description of her relationships, past and present, offers a way of understanding early attachment patterns as well as emerging potential.

The next piece involves two stories; a man who is at his wits end because of the tyrannical hold obsessive thoughts and compulsive actions have over him, and a woman whose life is being paralysed by agoraphobia. In my work with them it soon became clear that both their different symptoms were expressions of profound separation anxiety that transferred itself to an intense and idealised longing for times past.

Nostalgia

A young man comes to see me because he is tyrannised by an obsessive need to keep his house spotless. This has been going on for some while; although time-consuming, the compulsion has been just about manageable, but recently he has started to door check and increasingly feels the need to return home on the way to work, which has become practically as well as emotionally untenable. It is this behaviour that has driven him to seek help.

As he talks about his work, family, and relationships, I am struck by how often he refers to his childhood home with a mood of long-ing and nostalgia. Also striking is how often he aligns himself with his parents' opinions and beliefs, setting himself against his other siblings whom he describes as self-centred and thoughtless. During one session he puzzles over the fact that although he often longs to be at home with his parents to the extent that he often feels home-sick, he has just returned from a weekend at the family house and as happens so often, he felt restless and irritable. Once back at the old childhood home for any length of time, he is, confusingly, often overwhelmed by a desire to get away.

Homesickness, or waves of longing for something felt to be lost, is a common enough experience at various stages in life. Patterned into myths as the Eden or Paradise from which we inevitably fall, it can be understood psychologically as a longing for freedom from the inevitable difficulty we experience as we struggle to become our separate selves. Woody Allen's film *Midnight in Paris* is a sweet and witty exploration of how this nostalgic longing for a past Golden Age occurs when our experience of life is one of unacknowledged conflict and unhappiness.

Every child needs to eat from the tree of their own knowledge, yet because this facilitates emotional separateness every child feels it is complicated, prohibited. The forbidden apple is a symbol of choice and conflict, of desire for something that moves us away from the early breast comfort and fusion with the known. By reaching to take this emotional freedom we have to loosen our dependence on our earliest source of love, and the path to separation is often fraught with the pain of both needy compliance and angry defiance.

Winnicott once wrote about a boy he worked with who was obsessed with string. He would tie objects together all the time, chairs to tables, tables to cushions, cushions to fireplaces. Ever since he was very young, this boy's mother had been frequently hospitalised and Winnicott interpreted the string play as an expression of the boy's fear of separation. It wasn't safe to let go and venture forth alone.

Sometimes, unlike Winnicott's young patient, it is a surfeit of parental presence rather than the trauma of absence which prevents the cord being cut, the apple eaten. The young man obsessed with cleanliness had witnessed a great deal of parental anger and rejection when his siblings had munched the forbidden fruit. Terrified of a similar outburst of criticism, he had chosen to tow the parental line. But the cost was heavy. Love was conditional upon compliance and lack of separateness. His feverish need for order was his unconscious way of trying to ward off underlying anger and anxiety.

Developing our capacity to find our own way forward rather than follow the way shown to us by others is usually a slow and complicated process. I once worked with a woman whose request for a meeting was prompted by her recent experience of agoraphobia. She was deeply in love, soon to be married, and didn't understand why she had become utterly terrified of open spaces. When asked about her background, she described a very close-knit religious community. She told me how her parents had always expected her to marry within this and didn't hide their disappointment when they learned she had chosen someone from a very different background.

Unlike the young man, this woman had dared to follow, and take pleasure in, the promptings of her own heart rather than obey the parental creed. It was the aftermath of her decision that she couldn't cope with. Engagement to someone "other" meant disengagement from all that was familiar. In my consulting room she began to paint an idealised picture of her childhood, one that she longed for and feared she had excluded herself from forever. It is perhaps not surprising that her phobia started shortly after she told her parents of her engagement.

For both these people, nostalgia and longing for a child-like state was a response to the pain and conflict of becoming separate. Whatever our early environment, it's a mood that most of us can probably identify with. In the daily struggle between our desire for belonging and our need for individuality, we probably all know the irritability that comes with too much compliance as well as the fear that can accompany the responsibility of making our own decisions.

Psychoanalysis is clear on this issue. Conflict and separation are part of what it means to be human. Longing for paradise is avoidance of the need to become healthily separate and make choices that come from our own needs. As soon as the hero in Woody Allen's film had chosen to end the relationship that was making him unhappy he was released from his nostalgic longing to return to a Golden Age. His capacity to express himself less compliantly and more authentically, or less safely and more freely, is rewarded in suitable Hollywood style by him falling in love. As psychoanalysis tells us, learning how to tolerate separation fundamentally involves learning how to love, as mature love is about the coming together of essentially separate and unique individuals.

Separation anxiety: I-It or I-Thou?

The simple and extraordinary fact of having being born at all means that we have all experienced separation anxiety because the fact of birth means we have all lost the experience of merged safety that intrauterine existence provides. From early on in our lives we experience the difficult tension between narcissistically using others to get what we need and letting ourselves be used in order to avoid feeling abandoned. Ideally, awareness that others are essentially different from us gradually develops into the capacity to show loving concern rather than only be preoccupied with our own hungers. The next piece illustrates how an inability to see the other as just that—essentially other—gets in the way of developing the capacity for equal and loving relationships.

A middle aged woman comes to see me because she feels swamped by a pervasive mood of anxiety. She is married, and talks about her husband in a tone of irritability and criticism. He never seems to do anything quite right, and she is aware that she continually falls into a pattern of control and nagging. Yet if her husband is ever physically absent, she feels utterly bereft, becoming panicky until his return.

A young man comes to see me full of despair about the ending of an umpteenth relationship. He falls in love easily, he explains, in fact he's never out of a relationship for long, but it always goes wrong. And he doesn't understand why. As he talks, a pattern emerges of his over-eagerness to please during the early honeymoon days, shifting to a feeling of resentment at always having to do what someone else wants. Love dissolves into a claustrophobic feeling of imprisonment and he becomes emotionally withdrawn, until he falls in love again and the whole cycle repeats itself.

Although the life stories of both these people are utterly different, they each struggle with separation anxiety, or an inability to be comfortably oneself in the presence of another without needing to either control or be controlled. Although experiencing their anxieties differently, they had both experienced deep difficulty with early attachments.

The middle-aged woman was left at a very early age with a series of continually changing nannies, as both her parents were often away. It wasn't safe to become attached to anyone, as they so often disappeared. As a result, her energy went in to making people do what she wanted them to do so that she could feel in control of her ever-changing world, yet she was rarely able to trust and love them as essentially separate persons in their own right. Expressions of difference and distance, whether through disagreement or actual physical absence, were always felt as the terror of abandonment.

The young man, on the other hand, was the eldest child of a very dominating mother, and he learnt early on that love was dependent upon towing the maternal line. Compliance was fostered, self-expression curbed, and the art of fitting in, rather than loving, developed. But it was at a great cost. Moments of feeling truly alive only came with the short-lived uncomplicated bliss of falling in love or through acts of secret rebellion against a controlling partner. So the pattern described above, of fitting in order to secure love, followed by the feeling of being trapped and needing to escape, was set in place early on.

In my consulting room, both these ways of warding off anxiety were expressed. The young man was painfully eager to please and agreed too readily with all I said, whereas the woman would habitually disagree with me, only to repeat my comment a few minutes later as if it was her own. For each of them, I was inadvertently embroiled in a way of relating fostered during their early childhood.

We can probably all recognise these patterns of controlling or being controlled as ways of dealing with separation anxiety. Complaints about people not doing what we want them to do, or resentment at being coerced into doing something we didn't really want to do, are as common as autumn leaves. Parents who mould children into repeating their own image and likeness, couples whose mannerisms and even clothes echo each other, and friendships that covertly depend upon agreement and compliance are all part of the same avoidance of facing the existential terrors that can come from feeling deeply alone.

Myself, my many selves

We tend to caricature people into types: someone is predominantly sadistic (bullishly controlling of others) or masochistic (submissively allowing themselves to be controlled). And yet we don't need to read a Virginia Woolf novel to know that the emotional life of any individual is continually full of inconsistency and changeability. As Meltzer put it: "Once we have abandoned the idea of a unity of the mind it becomes rather a crowded cave" (Meltzer, 1992, p. 114). What is relevant to health is how we deal with the motley crowds in our own particular cave; whether we try and organise them boot camp style, deny the existence of the ones lurking in the dark, or even, occasionally, enjoy the possibility of partying.

The next story is about a young woman's panic at internal inconsistency. Like so many people in therapy, she often described herself as an absence more than presence: "I don't feel I am being myself," she would say, or "I don't know who I am anymore," as if there had been a time of "more" that had become lost or not yet found. She talked of how she didn't know how to be in relationships without feeling sapped of her sense of self. When this happened she would retreat into shutdown mode. Many of her relationships were based on a predominantly false self structure so that although she sought others out to avoid an inner emptiness. Her longing for intimacy was never met or nourished.

> It is a warm summer afternoon yet the young woman in the consulting room appears cold, clenched up into herself, taut and withdrawn. It would be difficult to guess her age. She is in fact in her early twenties, but could easily be mistaken for being either a lot younger or a lot older. There is something unbearably sad about her unreachableness. Sitting with her, I feel a longing to kindle some warmth and liveliness in her, and wonder whether the wish for warmth is in part a way of protecting myself from the terrible experience of her faraway coldness. I try to stay with it, and now it feels like a rock face, and I think about how being with her often feels so rock- like.
>
> A song comes to mind. Simon and Garfunkel's "I am a Rock". After a few minutes I decide to mention it. She says she thinks she knows it, but is uncertain. She asks me how it goes and knowing it well I recall a few lines: "I am shielded in my armour, hiding in my room, I touch no one, and no one touches me. I am a rock, I am an island. And a rock feels no pain. And an island never cries." A painful and poignant silence fills the room. After a few minutes, I realise that her cheeks are wet. Silently, and with an uncanny stillness, she is crying.
>
> Many years ago I came across a poem by Blake called "The Clod and the Pebble". Briefly, the poem describes two ways of relating to the world. The first is described by Blake as being like a clod of earth: malleable, self-sacrificing, and easily moulded to accommodate external pressures. The other way he describes as

being pebble-like: stalwart, ruthless, and seemingly impervious to the external tide of demands.

When I first read the poem I thought of these two ways as belonging to very different kinds of people: those who are eager to please in a clod-like, mortar-between-the-bricks way; and the pebble-like unbudging sort of person who seldom does what they don't want to do. At some point I began to realise that far from representing opposite kinds of people, being clod or pebble-like is invariably about the different ways any one individual responds to needs and fears.

Take, for example, the young woman above. I had first met her about five years previously when she was about to go to university. We had worked together for a few months, and then I hadn't seen or heard from her from that day to this. I felt shocked by the change in her, as five years before she had been far from pebble-like. If any-thing, her problem had been the opposite as she had been painfully eager to please, accommodating herself to others needs to a deeply confusing degree. Like the clod in Blake's poem, this too-passive, too-giving stance had lead to her experiencing a terrifying kind of inner formlessness. I remembered her telling me then that she felt she was everyone and yet somehow no one.

Somewhere along the line during her early months at univer-sity something inside of her had buckled. In pleasing everyone and feeling no one, she had stretched herself so thinly that her body and mind instinctively and necessarily went into shutdown mode. Without thinking about why she was doing what she was doing, she went into retreat, battened down the hatches, and became the withdrawn person that was sitting with me in the room.

A little like those with some degree of autism, anorexia, and psy-chosis, hers was an extreme retreat from what was experienced as an unmanageable world. In the world of relationships she had been all mortar without the bricks, and, under any pressure, the inner structure couldn't hold.

I suspect many people are familiar with a similar, if less pronounced, vacillation. Many of us know the feeling of inner emptiness which follows being too over-accommodating, and the loneliness which can accompany a defensive retreat from relationships. Both of these clod and pebble reactions are just that: needy, frightened, and angry reactions to the inevitable complications of our relationships with others.

Oedipus: the tragedy of trying to control the uncontrollable

Attempting to try and control our fears by controlling ourselves and each other is at the centre of the most famous story in psychoanalysis. Based on the play by Sophocles, Freud's interpretation of the Oedipus myth can (despite its sexist, normative, and homophobic limitations, which I explore in Chapter Five) be a useful metaphor for exploring how desire for deep intimacy can be experienced as dangerous, and how the ways we try to ward off the anxiety triggered by this desire means that we are always on the run from what we long to have.

> A man comes to therapy because for about a year he has been suffering from sexual impotence. In his thirties, and seemingly happily married, shame and sexual frustration are obviously taking their toll. Over time, the jigsaw pieces of his early relations begin to create a coherent picture. An only child, he was utterly adored by his charismatic and strong-willed mother. Between his parents there was always acrimony and bickering. His father, a rather henpecked, submissive man always received his wife's disparagement without a fight. My patient grew up resentful rather than respectful of his father, and deeply embroiled in his mother's need for him to be the apple of her eye.
>
> Emotional separation from his mother never really happened. Marriage enabled him to put some distance between them but, as his wife once remarked, it always felt as if there were three of them in the home. Unable to stand up to his mother's continual engulfing and controlling demands, my patient became more and more like his submissive father. Increasingly frustrated by his passivity, his wife inevitably began to sound more and more like his disparaging mother.
>
> A few years into their marriage, his sexual impotence became a problem. Until then, sexual relations between them had been loving and satisfying. With this new bodily humiliation and frustration my patient's emotional passivity worsened. He tellingly came to therapy at the request of his wife. "Tell your therapist,"

she had said, "that it's Oedipal, because it's all about your mother."

At one level she was right. But what does it mean? The term "Oedipal complex" is bandied about with the ease of a platitude as if we are all familiar with what Freud meant by it. But are we? Is it really about little boys wanting to have sex with their mothers and kill their fathers? And if it is as universal as Freud believed, what relevance does it have for each and every one of us in our everyday lives?

The term was coined by Freud whilst he was embarking upon his own self-analysis. Associations to his own dreams led him to early memories, including one which he wove into the ancient story by Sophocles and made into the bedrock (in every sense) of his new theory. The memory was of his early infatuation with his mother and jealousy of his father, and the theory this evolved into was, of course, the Oedipus complex.

In Sophocles' cycle of plays, Laius and Jocasta, the parents of Oedipus, are told that their son will one day kill his father and marry his mother. To avoid this fate, they abandon their son. Unknown to them, he is saved and raised by another couple. In time, Oedipus learns from another prophecy that he will kill his father and marry his mother. Believing his adoptive parents are his own, Oedipus flees from them to avoid acting out these lustful and murderous acts. Inevitably, tragically, he unknowingly does kill Laius, marry Jocasta, and so commits the murder and incest they have all been so afraid of.

Freud used the story to reinforce his belief that all of us, in our early years, experience both intensely erotic and hateful feelings towards our parents. Because full expression of such feelings is unthinkable, we learn to repress these emotions. Yet they often smoulder on unresolved, frequently fuelled by a parent's similar but unacknowledged feelings towards the child. A mother who is unhappy in her marriage may, as in the case above, draw libidinous pleasure from her son in a way that prevents his healthy separation. An emotionally absent father may, also as above, make the child feel both powerful and afraid that his desire to possess the mother may be possible.

As the child becomes adult, the intensity of these early feelings is repressed, yet the pattern of relationship established during infancy is often transferred to others in later life. For the man above, deep intimacy with his mother had always had an uncomfortable edge to it and as maternal feelings were increasingly transferred on to his wife, these early anxieties were re-activated. Impotence was his unconscious way of managing to maintain some vital degree of separateness in a pattern that felt too (s)mothering. To recover his own potency he needed to challenge his clearly unresolved Oedipal issues by standing up (in every sense) and relating with authority rather than with a carbon copy of his father's passivity (which was clearly sabotaging his own potential paternity).

Freud referred to this process as making "repetitions into memories" and it goes to the heart of what he believed the Oedipal story was about: we may often be driven by forces we don't understand which have their roots in our infantile emotions, but we can, through reflection, have a say in such habitual repetitions until they hopefully become at some stage as separate as a memory.

Between idea and reality

Insight, as Jung once wrote, needs to lead to endurance and action (Jung, 1973) but as we all know there is often quite a time lag between the start of an idea and our capacity to make it into reality. Hamlet's popularity is a reflection of our identification with this angst-filled space between intention and action. For the first part of the play we watch him sabotaged by an inability to translate insight into purposeful action (" … the Native hue of resolution/Is sicklied o'er with the pale cast of Thought"). When, later on in the play, he is able to integrate thought and resolution and so "suit the action to the word, the word to the action", the resulting potency energises and transforms him. Like the earlier Hamlet, the above man knew he was being passive-aggressive and that this paternal repetition wasn't helping him or his wife one jot, but standing up to his mother (as Hamlet finally did) and having to endure her response demanded more courage than he could muster.

We often prefer the Devil we know, even if that Devil is our own dysfunctional way of relating. Change involves giving something up as well as getting something new and if losing the approval of those we need is the price we have to pay, staying with the safety of the known is often the chosen option.

The next story is about how relationship choices can be an unconscious way of enabling us to remain stuck. Finding someone else with the same fears and anxieties is a useful way of letting yourself off the hook. This story is also about the difficulties involved when one of the parties makes a bid for change and freedom.

Two peas in a pod

The couple sitting in the room with me look at each other cautiously. This is our fourth session together, and not for the first time I am struck by their uncannily similar mannerisms and clothing which seem to blur any differences. Their cautious glances are tinged with anxiety. It is a big deal, sharing details of a private life with a virtual stranger. And perhaps the biggest deal of all is that some of the things being said have never been heard before by their "other half".

My patients are both in their mid-forties. They have only known each other a few years but have been married for a large part of that time. It was, they tell me, very much love at first sight. Both had been lonely. Both had found the world a difficult place to engage with. But now, with each other, they felt defended against the insecurities that dogged them.

Hearing about their early histories illuminates the causes of these anxieties. Between the ages of twelve and sixteen the woman had been sexually abused by her older stepbrother. Like so many victims of sexual abuse, she had kept this secret for too many years. When she did finally and courageously articulate her trauma, she was disbelieved and ridiculed by her family.

Her husband's insecurities originate from a less traumatic, but nevertheless deeply wounding, early environment. He was brought up by an unhappy mother who continually undermined him with criticism.

Because of their early experiences, neither had been able to sally forth easily into the world as confident individuals. Both had avoided relationships, preferring the safety of retreat to the risk of vulnerability and pain. Until one day they had found each other.

All had gone like a dream until a few months ago when what had felt so easy became horribly fraught and in danger of disintegration.

They both desperately wanted their marriage to work, and couldn't understand what was going wrong.

Each experienced the marital disharmony from a slightly different angle. For the husband, the early wonderful relief at no longer feeling lonely had recently given way to emotional claustrophobia. His wife, he confessed guiltily, had begun to irritate him. They spent all of every day together, and he longed for a bit of space. But even going for a short walk alone was taken by her as a sign that he no longer loved her.

He tried to ignore this rising claustrophobia because a lifetime of maternal criticism had taught him to muffle any potentially provocative remarks. But his wife had, of course, picked up on his unaired irritability. Terrified of losing what she had spent her life searching for, she had become clingy and needy, which only increased his sense of being trapped.

At the root of their mutual neediness and current distress was a misunderstanding about the nature of intimacy. As neither felt very robustly secure within themselves, they had found, within the other, solace from their own emotional fragility. Falling in love had flooded them with a wonderful sense of completeness, of being understood. But they had failed to move on from this stage of emotional merging and find room for the separateness that is so vital in any healthy relationship. The husband's need for some degree of solitude was a desire for healthy separateness. But it was experienced by him with guilt, and by his wife as a sign of rejection. They needed to trust that intimacy isn't about being two peas in a pod, but about two essentially different people coming together in love.

Cultural conformity versus individuality

Pressure to be on the same page as each other is often rooted in wider demands for social and cultural conformity. As the next story illustrates, trying to fit in with what is seen as "normal" can often derail a healthy sense of authenticity.

"I didn't even want to go. I'd have preferred to have the place to myself for the evening. But when they teased me about staying in all the time, I felt I had to prove there wasn't something wrong with me. So I went along, to join in. But I hated every minute. It felt phoney. And I felt boring and stupid and wooden, and couldn't think of anything to say to anyone. Everyone else around me was having a great time. Why couldn't I? Is there something wrong with me? I just felt like crying, and wanted to get back home."

The woman sitting in the chair opposite me looks frayed and anxious. In her late twenties, this is her second experience of therapy. The first was when she was at university, several years before. At that time, she had suffered a breakdown, taken time out, and bravely returned to complete her studies. From what I understood of this earlier history, she had weathered things far better after returning because of falling in love with another student. Similarly shy and reclusive, they had, like babes in the wood, protected each other from the relentlessly sociable demands of student life. Both of them were women and my patient, who had recognised her bisexuality a few years before, felt nervous about her parents' reaction to the relationship, so she always talked about her partner to her family as a university friend.

Recently this relationship had come to an end and although the decision to go separate ways had been hers, she felt unexpectedly fragile and lonely. Memories of her earlier breakdown began to trouble her. Her family were worried that she spent too much time alone, and she buckled under pressure from her mother to leave her solitary living quarters and move to a shared flat in order to try and "join in with life a bit more". At one level the move was a relief as it enabled her to avoid experiencing the terrors that moments of self-knowledge seemed to force her way.

The move was, however, very much from frying-pan to fire, as her flat mates, two women about her age, were ferociously sociable. Judging herself against their outward confidence and clear heterosexual identity, her loneliness increased. Anxious that she was in some way inadequate and missing out on life she began to force herself to join in with their clubbing habits, drinking binges, and lengthy comparisons of body shapes and sexual experiences. Her mother was glad she was joining in more, but every attempt to be "normal" left my patient feeling more troubled and lost.

About ninety years ago, Jung coined the terms introversion and extraversion to describe what he felt were fundamentally different personality types. Although far more complex than the simple distinction between preferring a quiet night in to being out partying, his definitions underline that introverts instinctively seek solitude when feeling ragged with stress whereas extraverts are always thirsty for stimulation and external relationship.

Unfortunately for my introverted and bisexual patient, our Western culture is hugely biased towards extraversion and hetero-sexuality. Many people feel insecure about being who they feel they are simply because the pressure to be otherwise is so forceful and widespread. As both her mother and sister were "life and soul of the party" extraverts, my patient often felt she was the cuckoo in the family. During her teenage years, she had gone through phases of trying to "join in", but this false self had inevitably failed and left her feeling even more alienated.

How do we explore, as therapists, the impact of social, cultural, and gender issues upon an individual's experience of herself? For the young woman above there was family, peer, and a more covert cultural pres-sure to mould her behaviour, sexuality, and looks into socially pre-scribed forms. She both longed to fit in and feel accepted and longed to discover how to live her life a different way. She didn't know whether to try to be like others or try to be like herself, and the tension precipi-tated a further breakdown.

As the next piece illustrates, people not only embody specific cul-tural expectations but also anxieties and terrors that have been uncon-sciously passed on from one generation to the next. The piece below describes how two experiences of phobia developed from very different histories of trauma and distress.

A man phones his wife in distress. She hurries home to find him huddled in a chair, shrunk in terror. He jabbers an explanation. A large spider crawled from the cupboard as he went to change clothes. It takes nearly an hour for him to relax enough to get up and on with the task of living.

A woman stands by the window in her hallway. She has a star-tled look, and her body is tense, her breathing shallow. She takes her coat from its peg, and is visibly shaking as she makes herself open the front door and leave the house.

Most of us know someone with some degree of phobic reaction to a specific object or situation. It may well be ourselves. Fears of flying, heights, mice, spiders, snakes, dogs, bats, enclosed spaces, open spaces, social situations, public speaking, the dark ... these are the commonest triggers of phobic reactions.

For many people the fear is just about manageable because just about avoidable. But not everyone is so lucky. For the agoraphobic woman above, the terror of venturing into open spaces thwarted her life on every front. She lost her job, her marriage fell apart, and her daily, lonely terror was soon accompanied by a severe depression.

There is little theoretical agreement over the origins of phobic terrors. The biological school of thought argues that, far from being irrational, phobias are leftovers from our evolutionary past. From our ancestors, the argument goes, we have inherited the instinctive knowledge to avoid snakes, be wary of animals, fear the dark. Another explanation is the trauma theory, the idea that a phobia can be tracked down to a specific fright. A man is afraid of dogs, for example, because he was bitten by one when very small.

Neither of these approaches fully explains phobic responses. The genetic approach leaves so many fears unexplained (how does it make evolutionary sense to be terrified of feathers or buttons?) and the trauma theory often doesn't fit with someone's history. Psychoanalytic theory, which looks at how fear is unconsciously absorbed from the world around us, offers what feels to me like a more convincing explanation.

Working with people whose lives are severely troubled by phobic reactions, there is frequently an underlying current of fear about losing control running through the narrative of their lives. Many describe how, from an early age, they have avoided situations that make them anxious. Many reel off a litany of phobias that have changed shape as they grew older. The agoraphobic woman above suffered as a child from a fear of the dark and of school. The man suffering from a terror of spiders had been petrified of pigeons as a boy. It is as if the phobic object or situation becomes a habitat for all the unnamed and uncomfortable feelings of fear. As Freud said: "Phobias have the character of a projection in that they replace an internal, instinctual danger by an external perceptual one."

Freud concentrated on listening to the patient's personal history to track down the origins of fear and avoidance. More recently, psychotherapeutic research has been casting the net into the wider culture. For example, recent studies have persuasively shown the effect that war trauma can have not only upon the victims themselves but on their children and their children's children.

The woman who suffered from agoraphobia was a "transgenerational" war victim (Pines, 2010). Her parents had endured unthinkable suffering during the Holocaust. They both physically survived the horrors of a concentration camp yet never talked openly to their daughter about the terror they had experienced. It was only after their deaths that she began to make sense of the shadow of fear that had haunted her childhood home. Without any knowledge of the origins of her anxieties, her body had absorbed her parents felt but unnamed terror and made it peculiarly her own.

Most phobias are less traumatic in origin, yet usually carry the same pattern. As children we both actively perceive our worlds and unconsciously absorb parental and cultural fears and prejudices, reshaping these into our own anxieties and terrors. The man above who suffered from arachnophobia remembered that his overanxious and unhappy mother had simply been afraid of everything. Like a baton in a relay race, she had unwittingly passed this fear on to her son who had in turn projected the irrational internalised anxiety on to his phobic terrors.

Speaking of our identities

As outlined at the start of this chapter, we are all born into a world of relationships, into a world of language. The connection between the intra-psychic and the wider social and political context is deeply present in the therapeutic experience because it is deeply present in an individual's experience of her own subjectivity. The stories we engage with as therapists are often significantly imbued with the insecurities and anxieties triggered by sexism, racism, homophobia, cultural, and class-based discriminations.

How do we recognise this contextual connection in our work? Or perhaps more importantly, *do* we recognise the intersubjective and relational aspects of any individual's experience. As Ellis and O'Connor argue in their exploration of race, class, gender and sexuality in *Questioning Identities*, "each human being is always more complex than can be encompassed by any one psychoanalytic framework" (Ellis & O'Connor, 2010, p. xiv).

Recognition of the uniqueness of others' differences in our work can only happen if we allow ourselves to be open to what we do not know, and to what our particular analytic theory does not prescribe. When we listen to someone's experience it doesn't come packaged with a label telling us where it's from, and sometimes, as in the example below, our preconceptions and expectations can block awareness of this.

> A successful business woman comes to therapy shortly after her father has died because she is feeling overwhelmed by loss and grief. As therapy gets under way it becomes clear that despite her comfortable lifestyle and successful work status she often feels deeply insecure about herself. She talks about how she enjoyed a very happy and materially comfortable childhood in Nigeria and moved with her close-knit family to London the year she became a teenager. Her insecurity and inferiority is almost palpable and I wonder how much it is connected to her recent loss. Her father had been immensely significant in her life. Then a few months after we had started working together she happens to mention that, when at her top private girls' school, she had suffered from intense and ongoing racism from a couple of the girls in her class. For years she had self-harmed, often thought of taking her own life, and felt deep shame in the colour of her skin.

I was left with the uncomfortable recognition that both her bereavement and the fact she embodied the kind of power and confidence that is often synonymous in our culture with material success, had made me myopic to the obvious possibility that it was racism that had left an internalised experience of powerlessness and insecurity in its wake.

The next chapter is about a specific cause of insecurity and internalised powerlessness for many women: sexual inequality. The cultural implications of our biological sex mean that there is no such thing as being born female without encountering sexual inequality. "The shadow of the object fell upon the ego" wrote Freud (Freud, 1917e), referring to mourning and melancholia. His words could just as easily refer to the shadow of the patriarchal object that, despite so many sociocultural and political changes, continues to fall on to, and constrict, the emotional lives of so many women.

References and suggested reading

Alayarian, A. (Ed.) (2007). *Resilience, Suffering, and Creativity: The Work of the Refugee Therapy Centre*. London: Karnac.

Benjamin, J. (1990). Recognition and destruction: An outline of intersubjectivity. In: S. A. Mitchell & L. Aron (Eds.), *Relational Psychoanalysis: The Emergence of a Tradition*. London: Analytic Press.

Bowlby, J. (1969). *Attachment and Loss*. London: Hogarth Press. (Reprinted: Pelican: Middlesex, 1987).

Dowrick, S. (1994). *Intimacy and Solitude*. London: The Women's Press.

Ellis, M. L. & O'Connor, N. (2010). *Questioning Identities: Philosophy in Psychoanalytic Practice*. London: Karnac.

Freud, S. (1917e). Mourning and Melancholia. *S.E. 14*. London: Hogarth Press.

Jung, C. G. (1973). *Jung Letters*. Vol. 1. (Bollingden Series. Eds. G. Adler and A. Jaffe. Trans. R. F. C. Hull). Princeton: Princeton University Press.

Klein, J. (1987). *Our Need for Others and its Roots in Infancy*. London: Tavistock. (Reprinted, London: Routledge, 1993).

Lacan, J. (1977). *The Four Fundamental Concepts of Psycho-Analysis*. London, Hogarth. (Reprinted London: Penguin, 1991).

Meltzer, D. (1992). The Claustrum. London: Karnac.

Pines, D. (2010). *A Woman's Unconscious Use of her Body*. Sussex: Routledge.

Skynner, R. & Cleese, J. (1983). *Families and How to Survive Them*. London: Methuen.

Strout, E (2008). *Olive Kitteridge*. London: Simon & Schuster. (A novel that powerfully communicates the complex relationship between what is shared and what remains hidden in relationships).

Waddell, M. (1998). *Inside Lives: Psychoanalysis and the Growth of the Personality*. London: Duckworth & Co. (Reprinted, London: Karnac, 2005).

Winnicott, D. W. (1964). *The Child, the Family and the Outside World*. London: Penguin.

Winnicott, D. W. (1974). Mirror-role of mother and family in child development. In: *Playing and Reality*. London: Penguin.

CHAPTER FIVE

The angel in the house

I am myself. That is not enough ...
What would the light
Do without eyes to knife, what would he
Do, do, do without me?

—Sylvia Plath

We all start our lives as female or male, girl or boy, and learn early on in childhood to identify with the gender stereotype that is assumed to correlate with our biological sex. This chapter explores how being born a girl, and internalising a culturally restrictive interpretation of feminine attributes, can significantly influence who we feel we are and how we love.

The stories in this chapter are limited to descriptions of heterosexual women. The exploration of women's different sexual identities and the history of psychoanalysis' response to homosexuality is cogently covered elsewhere (O'Connor & Ryan, 1993; Maguire, 1995). The parallel story to this chapter, the exploration of how men frequently internalise a limiting and rigid masculine identification, has similarly been explored by others elsewhere (Jukes, 2010).

Just like a woman

Like most therapists, I work with women of all ages, sexual orienta-
tions, and backgrounds and it has often struck me that, irrespective
of any personal differences, women's emotional lives are remarkably
alike. Compared to men, women are more concerned with looking after
the needs of others (especially when those others are men and children) than in looking after themselves. Additionally, when women are
given a chance to look after themselves (e.g., to speak for themselves
in therapy) they often find it difficult to turn the tables and receive the
attention and empathy they so readily give out to others (as patients,
for example, women are notorious for enquiring about the health and
wellbeing of their therapists).

Why is it that therapists, nurses, teachers, and carers are mostly
women? Why is it that when women get together they invariably talk
about the emotional intricacies of their lives, whilst men are more likely
to discuss work, politics, computers, sport? Are women just born with
a greater interest in the emotional needs of others or do they unconsciously collude with what is culturally expected of them?

What do women want?

Freud, perplexed by women's preoccupation with others' needs
rather than their own, once famously said that after thirty years of
studying the feminine soul he still didn't know what women want
(Freud, 1933). As explored in Chapter One, biological determinism
dominated Freud's thinking and he approached the gender issue
from the perspective that anatomy was destiny. His predominantly
deterministic approach to differences between men and women was
widely echoed amongst many of his contemporaries. Helen Deutch,
for example (a colleague of Freud's) believed that, simply by dint of
their biological sex, women are naturally more passive, submissive,
masochistic (Maguire, 1995).

Viginia Woolf and the angel of patriarchy

However, even at this time, radically different perspectives were being
voiced. Virginia Woolf (wife of Leonard Woolf whose Hogarth Press
publications of Freud's works made them accessible to the English pub-

lic for the first time) strongly rejected what she saw as the patriarchal root of psychoanalysis and its damagingly restrictive understanding of the feminine, a restriction that she perceived all around her. "The angel in the house" (Woolf, 1966) was Woolf's satirical description of women's self-sacrificing tendency to masochistically look after others needs. Her writing is full of manifestations of this angel's presence in her heroines' lives. Mrs Ramsey in *To the Lighthouse* is, for me, the most brilliant of her portraits of a woman's self-destructive selflessness. Writing about her own experience of this angel, Woolf says: "It was she who used to come between me and my paper, who bothered me and wasted my time and so tormented me that I killed her" (Woolf, 1966, p. 285).

Feminist perspectives

Today, many contemporary theorists agree that for many women this angel is regrettably still alive and kicking in many women's houses. Feminist analysts since the 1970s in Britain, the USA, and France (Benjamin, 1990; Chodorow, 1978; Eichenbaum & Orbach, 1982; Eichenbaum & Orbach, 1983; Irigaray, 1985a) have all offered differing perspectives in relation to women's subjectivity. The French psychoanalyst Luce Irigaray argues that Freud's theorising is such a patriarchal construction that it inevitably colludes with the very ways of speaking that prevent women from experiencing and expressing their own subjectivity. In Britain, in their critique of Freud's theorising, Orbach and Eichenbaum argue that girls, through sharing the same gender as their mothers, learn to prioritise others' needs above their own and to split off those experiences deemed to be "unfeminine" (e.g., their sexuality and their anger). As equality increases between the sexes and diverse forms of family structures challenge the constrictively normative, girls and boys, they argue, will be enabled to identify more fluidly with the characteristics currently attributed to one sex or the other.

Feminine and masculine: what does that mean?

Whatever each of us thinks about the theories, it is the ways we experience our own sex and gender identities as a man or a woman that is likely to determine how we respond to these issues in our work. If we are unconflicted about feminine and masculine, we are unlikely to interpret the normative in our patients' lives as potentially problematic. If we have experienced our gender identification as in any way restrictive and complicated, we are more likely to recognise the connection between, for example, a woman's hurts and hates and her understanding of herself as feminine.

Both/and or either/or?

The following thumbnail sketches illustrate how it is often through expressions of difference from the norm that we become more aware of invisible but invidious gender stereotypes.

A woman in her early forties is distraught following the end of a relationship. Her partner of fifteen years has left her because she has no strong desire to have children and because he felt threatened by her considerable power and success at work. She wrestled for years about the baby issue, but the idea of giving up the work that she loves fills her with dread, and she has met enough women during her working life to know that some kind of giving up is always required when children come on the scene. She is top of her tree and proud of her considerable achievement which has demanded a degree of ruthlessness that many would baulk at. She knows her ex found this very difficult, especially recently when he failed to get a promotion he badly wanted. As she talks she cries about the partner she deeply loves and misses, and asks me if I think there is something wrong with her: is she "unsexed", like Lady Macbeth, because she has no maternal longing?

A man in his late thirties has come to see me because of feeling conflicted about his job. He has twice turned down openings for promotion because of anxiety about the leadership qualities needed and the extra time commitment required. Although he enjoys his work he is aware that a lack of motivation to aim high lurks beneath his absence of drive. He has, he tells me, other things apart from work that matter, and he doesn't want to get too busy for these. He writes poetry, has had a small collection published, and would love to repeat this achievement, but the job thing worries him. Does lack of ambition make him less than a man? Extremely intuitive and empathic, he often puts others before himself. All sessions, for example, begin with him asking how I am, as if he is uncomfortable about taking the space for himself. And much of his time in therapy is taken up with him talking about his partner and children who are clearly and lovingly the centre of his world.

It is easy to use the terms masculine and feminine as some kind of givens, but what do they mean (and why do we usually talk of masculine "or" feminine rather than "and")? Although hugely variable between cultures and over time, in our own society many associate maleness with power, strength, logical thinking, law and order; femaleness with relatedness, intuition, spontaneity, strong feeling, nurturing.

Despite significant changes in recent years about gender roles, there still remains a widespread expectation in our culture that men should be more masculine and women more feminine, and both of the people described above unintentionally challenged aspects of that reductive opposition. In a positive sense they both had "more" because they were integrating elements of the usually separated notions of masculine and feminine behaviours, yet they both feel self critically "less" because anxious at being out of kilter with the norm.

Starting life the same?

Many therapists (including Freud and Jung) believe that at birth we are emotionally bisexual and that it is only gradually during childhood that the attributes ascribed to feminine and masculine become separated identities. Freud, who understood this shift, from inclusively experiencing both to exclusively identifying with one as natural and inevitable, explained it through the Oedipal complex. Put very simplistically, little boys grow to identify with the father's world of potency and power and, in order to achieve this, need to turn away from their mother's world of dangerously seductive but vulnerable feeling. Little girls on the other hand discover they lack a penis and, fuelled with envy, set about trying to win a man because they know they can't be one.

From today's view of things this looks insular and sexist, and of course a lot of challenges to both the Oedipal complex and Freud's version of gender differences are now on the map. Even way back in the 1920s, Karen Horney was arguing that male womb envy, not penis envy, was the big issue as it explained why men feel the need to dominate and denigrate women. More recent writing has focused on how psychotherapy too often colludes with, rather than challenges, the deterministic assumption that women are inherently hysterical, narcissistic, and masochistic. If you start from the premise that women's maladies are intrinsic to who they are, then belief that change is possible is unlikely to be on the agenda.

Sexual difference or sexual inequality?

So how does this translate into our work as therapists? If a patient is compliant in her relationships with men do we think it is because of her normal, inborn feminine passivity, or because, lacking a penis, she feels like a second-class citizen, or that she has learned to experience herself as inferior because of pervasive cultural sexual inequalities? Or can it be all of these? When is expression of sexual difference also an expression of sexual inequality?

Masochism, narcissism, and hysteria: the female maladies

Below are some examples of women with heterosexual gender identities behaving in ways that could describe the stereotypical female maladies of submissiveness, masochism, narcissism, and hysteria (Showalter, 1987). The first is a story about a woman who transferred on to her family life what she learned from her mother and father: the art of pouring all her energy into looking after her husband and nurturing her children in response for the comfort of feeling needed. The trouble was that however hard she looked after and loved others, no one, least of all herself, came out satisfied.

"To please everyone is spiritual death" (Milner, 1986, p. 94)

> Once upon a time there was a coquettish little princess of a girl who was utterly the apple of her father's eye. She learned early on how to dance to his tunes as the result was always a gratifying adoration. As she grew older, she met her own prince for whom she similarly became the object of desire. They married, had two children, and the little princess made herself indispensable in the way her own mother had and the way so many good women do, by enabling her husband's and children's worlds to run smoothly. All she asked for in return was to feel valued and adored. For a while this pattern of being mortar between the bricks, in order to feel secure, seemed to work flawlessly.

One day, as if a terrible spell had been cast upon the marriage, everything felt out of joint. Her children were growing up and no longer seemed to need her, and her one-time prince now responded with barely concealed irritation to complaints that she didn't feel deeply loved. The little princess was filled with a terrible insecurity. No longer needed by others, she felt worthless and empty. She sank into a depression, she started drinking too much, she flew into rages. But nothing that she did brought back the security of feeling that she was the apple of someone's eye. Then seemingly out of the blue her world fell apart. Her prince found another princess. Her castle became a prison and she was trapped inside.

At the heart of this story rests one of the most frequent problems brought by women to therapy. Learned by so many little girls so early on, it is the problem of nurturing others excessively and needily without knowing how to ask for any nourishing in return. It is as if an unspoken agreement happens early on in the lives of many women in which they unconsciously agree to hand over their power to men in return for feeling needed. "If I promise to make you feel adored by running round in circles and ignoring my own needs," the unconscious message goes, "will you in return promise to make me happy?"

Such women are "daddy's girls", daughters of the patriarchy who learn to let the angel into their house very early on in life. In an unhealthy restriction of the masculine/feminine qualities that exist within us all, feminine potential is distorted and straightjacketed into a submissive and needy kind of nurturing, and their undeveloped masculine attributes are projected on to their man.

It is often not until the castle has tumbled down that scrutiny of how they are living and loving begins. The fairy tale is over, the prince has gone, and the emptiness that has entered their lives is painful and poignant. "What did I do to deserve this?" asked one woman recently. "I gave him so much for so many years".

Reflecting on her situation it was clear that what she "did" for so many years was give, give, give, and become emptier and angrier inside because she didn't feel that she was being nourished by anything in return. "Looking back, I suppose I had the helpless-but-indispensible role down to a fine art, just as my mother had, and could manipulatively wrap everyone round my little finger with it. Until they, perhaps understandably, got fed up."

> For this woman, recognition that fear of her own hunger and aggression had made her frequently curb self-expression was the beginning of a break through. Loosening her dependence on the outside world to dish out her own needs, she began to feel more in touch with, rather than cut off from, her own deep-seated power.

In terms of psychopathology, the behaviour of the woman above could be described as both masochistic and narcissistic: by idealising her father and husband she was (like Echo in Ovid's story of Narcissus) clinging to relationships without knowing how to express her need for a different kind of return.

Bluebeard

There is another ancient story that powerfully describes how women attach themselves to men in order to avoid feeling the terror of their own separateness and so individuality. It is the story of Bluebeard (Pinkola Estés, 1993). In this tale, a young woman agrees to marry a man out of immature need and naivety rather than mature love, then discovers to her horror that he is in fact a wife murderer. Understood psychologically, the story is about how women become Bluebeard to themselves and harmfully lock up their own potency when they choose a partner to make them feel safe rather than deeply alive.

Jane Campion's film *The Piano* is a modern interpretation of this Bluebeard story and well worth watching for its insightful portrait of how the powerlessness that goes hand in hand with masochistic behaviour often communicates itself through bodily symptoms. Unhappy and mute in her marriage, Holly Hunter's character in the film becomes imprisoned and cut off from life because of her unequal relationship with her husband. She has no power in her husband's world and her muteness is her body's potent expression of her emotional pain. Like Cordelia in *King Lear*, her silence enables her to preserve her integrity. Her piano-playing is similarly a means of authentic self-expression because it doesn't trap her in the language of someone else's meaning.

Eating disorders: hysteria?

In the language of psychopathology, the film's portrayal of mutism could easily be interpreted as conversion hysteria, and many of the ways women unconsciously "talk" with their bodies to express unresolved conflicts have long been understood in terms of the "wandering uterus" pathology of hysteria. Nowadays, anorexia, bulimia, and self-harm are the more frequent ways women use their bodies to articulate what they can't talk about with words. In our current cultural epidemic of body-based problems, overeating, under eating, and obsessing and worrying about body size, is so much the norm that these physical manifestations of emotional distress are often not seen as problematic at all.

I experienced this form of denial when working for *Marie Claire* as "resident psychotherapist" (a kind of glorified agony aunt). Some of my work involved answering the usual kind of problem page questions, but sometimes I would meet with women for a "one-off" therapy session and write up a condensed version to give readers a flavour of the kinds of conversations that can happen in therapy. The reasons given by women for wanting a session were usually about relationships difficulties, sexual jealousies, work dilemmas, family issues. But on nearly every occasion, a destructive relationship with their bodies and food emerged as a problem. I would put this into the final piece, as it was a faithful part of each woman's experience. One day, one of the editors asked me to cut any mention of eating disorders as it was both too repetitive and out of keeping with the image of women the magazine wanted to promote.

She was right: it *was* worryingly repetitive, and of course the world of woman's magazines can't afford to look too closely at why the images of women it is overtly promoting are covertly contributing to another generation of eating-disordered and body-hating angel women. As the next story illustrates, as long as women identify with an image of themselves that restricts healthy expression of their own power and aggression, food obsessions will (like Bluebeard's mutilated wives) remain shamefully locked out of sight, and many women will simply accept an eating disorder as both a secret and an expected part of everyday life.

> A slim woman in her late forties has been coming to sessions for about ten months. She initially requested therapy because of feeling "stuck and blocked", saying she was at a crossroads in both her love life and work, and needed help with seeing the options. She has an intensity about her, and a perfectionism, which she talks about as both a help and hindrance.

One morning she arrives for a session looking shattered and tearful. For a while she talks about work difficulties that have been preoccupying her, then in mid-sentence breaks down and sobs. When she is a little calmer she tells me that something she had been keeping secret for a very long while has been found out. "I feel so ashamed," she explains, "because for years and years I've been hiding my problem with food. Even from myself, in a way. Last night I thought I was alone but my boyfriend had come home without me realising. I'd had a bad day and was doing what I sometimes do when I'm alone without even thinking about it: bingeing then making myself throw up. When I'd finished, there he was standing in the bathroom doorway, looking horrified."

This woman is one of many in our culture with a hidden eating disorder (officially known as EDNOS: eating disorders not otherwise specified). Like many others she is reluctant to let go of her secret, to acknowledge just how unhealthy for both mind and body it is. She managed to keep it hidden for so long because she did not want to perceive it as a problem. It wasn't even on the radar during our sessions until her cover had been blown by the unexpected return of her boyfriend.

The painfully skeletal body of someone with severe anorexia, or the overburdened frame of a compulsive eater, are both visible signs to the world of their inner distress. But for the woman above, and the many like her, a secretly managed regime of moderate self-starvation, combined with occasional bouts of bulimia or laxative abuse, enable her to maintain an obsessively and unhealthily controlled weight.

During the weeks following the exposure she tells me just how obsessed with food she has been for years. From the age of twelve she fixated on pictures of women in her mum's magazines, and started to agonise over what she had eaten, might eat, would like to eat. Her mum was usually on a diet so it was easy to join in. As Judith Butler says, one of the cruel ironies of patriarchy is that those who are already oppressed prepare the next generation for a similar fate (Butler, 1997). By the time she was sixteen she had dropped from ten to eight stone. Because her weight was never critically low she managed to persuade everyone that there wasn't a problem. She was just losing puppy fat. So began the fixation which dominated her life for the next thirty years.

Nowadays, if she gets through the day on only an apple without anyone noticing, she feels high. Her obsession with food has, up until now, been a private affair. The obsession is, she acknowledges, a torment, yet it also gives her a peculiar feeling of power, an illusory sense of being in control. She quotes Kate Moss as saying that nothing tastes so good as the feeling of being thin. She loves the feeling of secretly staying slim, it makes her feel powerful and in control, and she is reluctant to give up her secret way of achieving it. Like any change, the gains have to outweigh the losses for motivation to kick in, and for her that tilt hasn't yet happened.

Like Holly Hunter's muteness, this woman held on to her eating disorder with a defiant stubbornness. Like many symptoms, it dealt with two threats in one go: both preventing a return of the unbearable repressed and creating a short-lived fiction of power in her relationships with others. The next story is about a young woman whose neatly razor-marked arms mapped her temporary escapes from overwhelming stress, though this method of escape was also her entrapment.

Cultural or self-harming?

"… the tension gets unbearable, and all I can think about is the razor. When everything is just a huge scream inside of me, it's all I want to do … while I'm cutting there's just this swell of relief."

The words are those of the young woman in my consulting room, and they send a shiver down my spine. I've listened to descriptions of cutting more times than it's comfortable to remember. In my experience it is women, not men, who cut. And increasingly, it is young women barely out of girlhood.

The young woman opposite me is in her twenties. She started cutting when she was fourteen. Unlike many women who cut themselves, she has been no victim of physical, emotional, or sexual abuse. She tells me about a happy-enough sounding childhood. Apart from the usual dollop of sibling rivalry, some normal testing-out during adolescence, and a bit of homesickness when she moved away for the first time, her life story bears no scars that warrant the neat criss-cross of cuts secretly etched on to her arms. So why does she literally let rip?

She tells me she remembers the first time it happened as if it was yesterday. She was sitting in her bedroom "feeling like shit". She had a period. She had spots. She was revising for an exam she didn't understand and knew she would be put into a lower set if she didn't pass. The boy she fancied was in the top set. Her best friend was in the top set. They were both cleverer than her. She went to the bathroom, and seeing herself in the mirror, angrily squeezed a spot. It made it worse. She felt fit to burst with unspilled tension. She picked up the razor on the basin and, without thinking, cut into her arm. The relief was immediate and enormous.

Psychoanalytic theories about self-harm focus on how an early abusive experience becomes self-perpetuated. The violence that has been dealt out to the victim becomes the violence she repeats on herself. People who have been cut down, cut out, verbally abused by a cutting tongue, turn the anger inwards in a terrible misdirection of aggression. As a therapist I have certainly worked with women whose self-mutilation has been triggered by traumatic experiences of suffering and abuse. Their cutting frequently goes hand in hand with an eating disorder, and both symptoms can be as difficult to shift as any tenacious addiction.

But, increasingly, I am both meeting and hearing about teenagers who have more in common with the young woman above: seemingly trauma-free life histories, with cutting starting in their early to mid teens. A recent survey based on an anonymous school questionnaire suggests that the number is swelling into something of a national epidemic.

One common denominator, running like a seam through many of their stories, is an internalised and relentless pressure for perfectionism in all areas of life, with academic success and body image causing the most stress of all. Often these young women describe their teenage world as frenetic with internal and external pressures.

Freud's notion of "free-floating anxiety" comes to mind, as does the restless discontent of so much in our culture. Many youngsters have to sit through over one hundred exams before they finish school. They struggle with trying to fulfil the unrealistic expectations of their worlds that say it is possible to be perfect in both body and mind. Mix this up with the usual amount of insecurity, turbulence, and acting out that is normal to adolescence, add an "off day", and, like the young women's story above, you're left with the fit to burst pressure that triggers much of the current "school" cutting.

Most adolescents eventually outgrow self-harm along with their teenage wardrobes. But of course, as Freud knew so well, symptoms don't just disappear unless the underlying causes have been well and truly exorcised. The socially accepted habits that frequently replace cutting are less likely to cause parental alarm: overworking, overeating, over drinking, under eating, smoking, obsession with dieting, obsession with exercise, obsession with material success in its myriad of illusive forms. But aren't these simply a new set of symptoms, muted forms of the earlier anguished intensity?

When we feel shocked by the self-mutilation of this growing number of teenage girls maybe we need to stop and think. Maybe the causes are not only within and between the child and her family, but are to be found in the madness of our pressure-cookered and sexist world that from a frightening young age makes young women believe success depends upon looking like and achieving the impossible. Maybe we should acknowledge that this teenage epidemic of mutilation is self-harm with a bang, whereas we adults prefer to do it with a whimper.

Most therapists will be very familiar with the kinds of experiences described in the last few stories. How does each of us respond to these kinds of symptoms? What, if any, theories do we use to understand them? Is the woman whose marriage collapsed narcissistic? Is the woman with the hidden eating disorder an hysteric? And the self-harming perfectionist, does she epitomise women's masochism? And yet, as explored above, aren't these the terms coined by patriarchy to explain and contain women's madness (Irigaray, 1985b; Showalter, 1987)?

What the language of pathology (and patriarchy) leaves out

Maybe we'll never know, or never agree, just how much culture and psyche interact. Maybe not knowing and not agreeing doesn't matter. But if the masochistic self-harming that so clearly marks the bodies and minds of so many women today is at some level an expression not of innate sexual difference but sexual inequality, how can we move on from the litany of female pathologies and maladies that, as therapists, we've all been nursed in? How does language move (and so move us) on? The next piece explores how being open to new experience necessarily diminishes the relevance of established meaning.

The use of words to communicate what we feel is always a double-edged tool. In therapy, people struggle to find a language to articulate experience. Wrestling to make verbal sense of what feels non-sensical is one way of taking control of our chaotic and uncertain worlds. It's what Adam did when he named the beasts in the garden of Eden. Once defined they were mastered, known, and so less fearful.

Eve wasn't part of this process of mastery. Adam's silent helpmate, she was watching from the sidelines, being defined by, rather than doing the defining. Her place in this particular story of Creation is an important reminder that the nature of the beast is always more than the definition that tries to capture it. If Eve had been given a speaking part in this story, she would have told a different version, found another way of naming the meaning of things.

As therapists, how do we ensure that patients have their own speaking part, that we don't impose our own meanings on to their stories, using language to explain to rather than explore with? The use of pathologies to understand emotional distress is a regular happening in psychoanalysis and psychiatry, and yet pathology is inevitably exclusive and generalising rather than particular and unique. It also creates the damaging illusion that something is fixed and prescriptive. Working with someone who has been told somewhere along the line that they "have" depression, or an addictive personality or schizophrenia or a borderline personality disorder, can be immensely destructive to the process of positive change.

This flaw in pathological description is clearly illustrated in the ways predictive and prescriptive language changes its use. The history of the term "perversion", for example, is a clear example of how various therapists have used the same term to describe very different manifestations of the emotionally problematic over time.

For Freud, perversion described a deviation from the "sexual aim", that is, genital intercourse and sexual reproduction and, until recently, acts of perversion (such as fetishism and exhibitionism) have been understood as predominantly male. As O'Connor and

Ryan (1993) have shown, Freud's initial writing on perversion was often incorrectly extended to homosexuality, and contemporary psychotherapists have increasingly challenged the subsequent pathologising by psychoanalysis of lesbianism and homosexuality.

But some psychotherapists have recently argued that women can also suffer from forms of perversion, not in the ways usually associated with men (sex addiction, pornography, fetishism) but in what have traditionally been understood as the masochistic and hysterical litany of female maladies, so the kinds of behaviours illustrated above in the stories of anorexia, bulimia, and self harm. Men, the argument goes, tend to use their external worlds to objectively release sexualised aggression whereas women, who have not internalised masculine ways of exhibiting power and control, turn their aggression inwards to their own bodies.

(Welldon, 1992)

How helpful are these new ways of describing distressing behaviours to the individuals we work with? Does it matter to any of the women mentioned above whether their behaviour is labelled as hysterical, masochistic, or perverse? Doesn't all psychopathology essentially enable us to distance ourselves from the person we are with, and so protect ourselves from engaging with the discomfort of her distress?

What this history of perversion does introduce is the question running through every story so far described in this chapter, namely: why is it that women so often feel the need to harm themselves (whilst, as the history of war and genocide illustrates, men tend to harm each other)? Welldon explains this difference through sexual inequality: "The perverse (self-harming) woman feels she has not been allowed to enjoy a sense of her own development as a separate individual, with her own identity, in other words she has not experienced the freedom to be herself" (Welldon, 1992, p. 8). In this reading of things, women self-harm because, like Holly Hunter's powerful mutism, their bodies are communicating what their gender identification has excluded them from healthily expressing from inside out.

Given that psychoanalysis is steeped in the language of patriarchy, this link between self-harm and culturally restrictive constructs of feminine identity is inevitably problematic for any therapist. No act of speech is ever neutral (Irigaray, 1985b), so how do we ensure that we are not unconsciously colluding with the language that has stifled so many women's subjective expression and so, inadvertently, perpetuating the distress they have come to therapy to understand? How do we know whether it is the patient or only an echo of our own language that we have heard? The next piece explores these questions through the story of a young woman who was severely ill with an eating disorder.

Disembodying or embodying language

Psychotherapy is often referred to as the "talking cure", and yet words can sometimes hinder, more than help, in the therapeutic process. As explored in Chapter Three, people often spend years developing the capacity to hide from both themselves and others, and speech is one way of continuing not to be found. As illustrated earlier, women consumed by an eating disorder often use words to avoid openly addressing their enslavement to food. There is both a longing for "cure" and a terror that this will mean the loss of what is needed. As one young woman said to me years after nearly dying from anorexia: "If I had told you just how much I still obsessed about food and tricked people into thinking I was returning to normal, it would have been a betrayal of the one thing I needed above all else. I wasn't ready to abandon the illness. It was still more friend than foe."

Working with someone with an eating disorder can therefore involve a particular focus on what is being felt more than what is being told, as verbal reassurances that progress is being made rarely include this painful complexity of denial. But if the illness is making someone dangerously ill, this attention to the nuances of the unsaid can become eclipsed by massive anxiety and a longing to take over in order to make sure someone does not die. Practical action is taken, other professionals are contacted, and we all try and "do" something to take control of the life-threatening behaviour. In these kinds of times, in the life and death reality of illness, a different kind of communication, which is more prescriptive and explanatory than mutual and exploratory, often dominates.

If working with someone who continually masks the truth of an addictive illness with the empty speech of reassurance can feel unsettling, living with them on a day to day level must, at times, feel well-nigh impossible. I remember several years ago meeting a woman whose daughter was in the iron grip of anorexia. She had come to see me because her daughter refused help of any kind and she herself was at the end of her tether. She had tried so hard, she told me, to be patient and understanding, but it had become an ugly battle of wills.

She resented her daughter's secrecy, worried terribly about her skeletal frame, and did not understand why she would not just listen to reason. She was terrified her daughter was going to die, and had developed a custodial approach to try and take control of the situation. Watching over her in the kitchen until she had eaten, weighing her several times a day, listening at the bedroom door for any sign of manic exercise and at the bathroom door for the sounds of vomiting, she was a detective in her own home. Their relationship deteriorated, her daughter stayed waif thin and she felt full of anger and remorse. What could she do or say to her daughter to make her give up this life-threatening madness?

I remember how her description of their "battle of wills" worried me. People suffering from anorexia often respond to cajoling and coercing by digging their heels even more firmly in. So if logic and reasoning only leads to a locking of horns and worsening of relations, what can help? How is it possible, in times of acute crisis as well as chronic unhappiness, to trust in what someone already has, instead of feeling the need to take control and tell them what to do?

Soon after meeting this woman, I came across a book called *To Die For*, an account of anorexia co-authored by the godmother (Carol) of the young woman battling with the illness (Emma). Emma lived with Carol for some time when she was ill and numerous extracts from Emma's food-obsessed diaries are slotted into Carol's narrative of the events. What emerges is a stark contrast between the raw honesty of Emma's self-reflective diary and the "warding off" language she uses with doctors, therapists, family, and even towards her much-loved godmother.

Like the mother above, Emma's godmother is often reduced to anger, frustration, and confusion by the secrecy and withholding. But although often exasperated by Emma's bizarre and potentially very dangerous eating habits, she manages (maybe because she is not the mother) to avoid the language of confrontation. "Perhaps surprisingly, Emma and I talk very little about her food," she writes. Instead, she feeds Emma with what she calls "the other kind of food". Music, laughter, books, nature, friendship, trust, love.

Over time Emma recovers, becomes hungry for life and embraces her place in it. Yet the moral of this story is that it was not any words of sense or reasoning which enabled her to move away from her illness. It was not a victory that emerged from a battle of wills. It was by being offered experiences of liveliness and love rather than distrust and control, connecting to a language of Eros more than Thanatos, that enabled life to win the day.

Most of the women described in this chapter felt, like Emma, disassociated from their bodies. Mutilated, starved, attacked, and criticised, their bodies were experienced as hated objects, disowned rather than loved, lived, and owned. As Eichbaumn and Orbach say: "The complex cultural attitudes towards women's bodies—that they are sexual, ugly, mysterious, extraordinary, dark, bloody and smelly—find a place in each woman's sense of her self" (1982, p. 40).

Attending from the inside

However much this body-hatred is part of a woman's relationship with herself, it is often not the overt reason for her coming to therapy. Often the focus is on relationships and life in general and why happiness is elusive. How do we, as therapists, find a way of bringing the often-neglected body into speech? How do we communicate in a language that (like Carol's to Emma) facilitates an experience of embodiment not disassociation, a way of living with love rather than hatred towards oneself?

Winnicott describes such reparation as being enabled by regression to an earlier experience of primary maternal preoccupation, an experience of feeling deeply and non-intrusively held by the other's unconditional and trusting acceptance (Winnicott, 1956). I think this is the kind of experience Milner is describing in her work with Susan quoted in Chapter One (Milner, 1988, p. 42) and what Irigaray means when she describes the potential of analysis as

opening or enigma, rather than as peremptory imposition of the
authority of a word, language or text ... For this to be a possible
alternative, the analyst must always keep in mind the dimension
of his or her own transference, must always remain close to yet
distant from the one to whom he or she listens ... reversible and
open, linking up all possible positions in space and time.

(Irigaray, 1985b, pp. 246–246)

The following story is about how a patient's neglected body unexpectedly came to be experienced as more owned than disowned in the therapeutic space.

A woman in her early thirties has been coming to therapy for a few
months. She is preoccupied about being recently "dumped" by her
boyfriend. She has a lot on her mind and doesn't find it difficult
to rapidly fill me in with a large quantity of emotional and bio-
graphical material. I pride myself on having a fairly good memory,
and start the process of trying to both absorb and sort the welter of
detail that is hurtling my way.

She tells me that although she feels hurt she is having sex with a
lot of different men as a kind of revenge and anyway it is her way of
getting over rejection. She speaks quickly and with a brittle kind of
bravery, and there is a look on her face of bone-china fragility that
unexpectedly moves me.

This sense of her fragility contrasts with the harshness of the
sexual encounters she is describing and I find myself wondering
about this undercurrent of vulnerability. As this is happening,
I become a little detached from her words (they kind of fly past
me now) and I stop trying to follow and fit together the speedy
fragments of her narrative.

A shaft of sunlight suddenly enters the room and illuminates her
body. It is as if I needed that spotlight. Slumped, inert in the chair,
I seem to notice her physicality for the first time. Her body appears
almost lifeless, a strangely muted appendage to her fast and fran-
tic flow of words that are full of the descriptions of sexual activities. I feel moved by its lost, uncared-for aura, and a different sense
comes to mind about her stories, a sense of the searing sadness of the
emotional abandonments she has suffered, losses that I know a little
about but which had at some level failed to reach me until now.

As if in response to what I was experiencing this woman said, quite unprompted: "My body never feels alive. Sometimes I stare at it in the bath and it feels like the body of a stranger."

Through this overlap of our separate reveries, what had been shamefully rejected was able to become a conscious part of the work, and proved to be a catalyst for significant shifts that emerged over the next months. The moment of connection between us had somehow enabled a new language to enter the room, a way of exploring how she retreated from emotional pain, the shame and disassociation she felt during sex, the gap between the body she kept abandoning, and her longing to feel connected to the woman she ached to become.

For Marion Milner, learning how to move with love for the body became her deepest preoccupation. Only then, believed Milner, can we properly love others and care for the wider world around. "Reintegration" was the term she used to describe the struggle towards "one's sense of being alive and inhabiting one's own body". "It seems," she wrote in one of her diaries, "as if one has to create one's body in some way, by attending to it from inside … The odd paradox is that by centring oneself one in fact gets more in touch with what's outside, not less."

The words of the young woman above ("my body never feels alive") are often echoed by women in therapy. Anxiously preoccupied about whether their body is "good enough", women often describe their physicality with a critical attention that is outside in. A woman who has recently fallen in love is full of how happy she is, then suddenly lets slip that during sex she is never "in" her body, but always watching from the outside, thinking about how her boyfriend will be seeing her. Another woman can only have sex when her body is covered by a duvet and the light is turned off, and even then she can't stop thinking about how repulsive she must look to her partner.

Some of the ways that therapy can facilitate a sense of aliveness by (in Milner's words) attending to the body "from inside" (Milner, 1973, p. 268) is the subject of the next chapter. For many women this process involves taking back some of the power and potential of their unowned masculine selves. For many men this involves owning some of the vulnerability and emotional complexity they habitually project on to women. For both sexes it is about breaking down limiting divisions between feminine and masculine, and so becoming more able to tolerate differences between, and possibilities within, our always shifting selves.

References and suggested reading

Benjamin, J. (1990). Recognition and destruction: an outline of intersubjectivity. In S. Mitchell and A. Aron (Eds.), *Relational Psychoanalysis, the Emergence of a Tradition.* Hillsdale, NJ: The Analytic press, 1999.

Benjamin, J. (1998). *The Bonds of Love.* New York: Pantheon.

Buckroyd, J. (1989). *Eating Your Heart Out.* London: Random House.

Butler, J. (1997). *The Psychic Life of Power.* California: Stanford.

Chodorow, N. (1978). *The Reproduction of Mothering.* Berkley, LA and London: University of California Press.

Eichenbaum, L. & Orbach, S. (1982). *Outside In … Inside Out.* Harmondsworth: Penguin.

Eichenbaum, L. & Orbach, S. (1983). *What Do Women Want?* Glasgow: Fontana.

Freud, S. (1905a). *Three Essays on the Therory of Sexuality* (Penguin Freud Library 7, 1991). Harmondsworth: Penguin.

Freud, S. (1933). Femininity. In: *New Introductory Lectures* (Penguin Freud Library 2, 1973). Harmondsworth: Penguin.

Hornbacher, M. (1998). *Wasted.* UK: Flamingo Press. (A compelling autobiographical account of an eating disorder.)

Irigaray, L. (1985a). *This Sex Which Is Not One* (Trans. C. Porter). Ithaca, NY: Cornell University Press.

Irigaray, L. (1985b). *To Speak is Never Neutral* (Trans. Schwab). London and New York: Continuum.

Jukes, A. (2010). *Is There a Cure for Masculinity?* London: Free Association Books.

Lee, C. (2004). *To Die For.* London: Random House.

Maguire, M. (1995). *Men, Women, Passion and Power.* London and New York: Routledge.

Milner, M. (1973). Some notes on psychoanalytic ideas about mysticism. In: *The Suppressed Madness of Sane Men.* London: Routledge, 1987.

Milner, M. (1986). *An Experiment in Leisure.* London: Virago.

Milner, M. (1987). *Eternity's Sunrise.* London: Virago.

Milner, M. (1988). *The Hands of the Living God.* London: Virago Press.

O'Connor, N. & Ryan, J. (1993). *Wild Desires and Mistaken Identities, Lesbianism and Psychoanalysis.* London: Virago and New York. (Reprinted New York, Columbia University Press, 1994; London: Karnac, 2003).

Pinkola Estés, C. (1993). *Women Who Run With the Wolves*. London: Rider.

Showalter, E. (1987). *The Female Malady: Women, Madness and English Culture*. London: Virago.

Welldon, E. V. (1992). *Mother, Madonna, Whore: The Idealisation and Denigration of Motherhood*. New York: Other Press.

Winnicott, D. W. (1956). Primary maternal preoccupation. In: *The Maturational Process and the Facilitating Environment*. London: Hogarth Press, 1990.

Woolf, V. (1966). Professions for women. In: *Collected Essays*. London: Hogarth Press.

CHAPTER SIX

I, me, myself, my selves

"The question is," said Alice, "whether you can make words mean so many different things."

—Lewis Carroll, *Through the Looking Glass*

Therapy often begins with a statement of loss, absence, death: "I feel as if I don't know who I am anymore", "I feel dead inside", "I'm not really living from me", "Life feels pointless and empty", "I feel so stuck", "People say 'just be yourself' but I don't know what my self is", "I have lost my soul" … these are the kinds of descriptions familiar to any psychotherapist. Yet when someone makes the decision to tell their story to a therapist it is because however lost, bleak, and empty they feel, somewhere deep inside of them is a hunger to feel alive again, and a hope, however small, that this is possible.

Expressions of profound emptiness like those described above often emerge from experiences of traumatic abandonment or intrusive engulfment in which a capacity to communicate from "a feeling of real" (Winnicott, 1956, p. 303) has become lost within mimicry of others. As explored in Chapter Three, this is partly to keep True Self experiences

109

safe from further threat. It is also a means of finding an identity and so a way of being heard.

Because of this there is often a sense of someone not knowing how to speak from themselves in the earlier stages of therapy. Words flail around, there and everywhere but never quite fully *here*, and there can be an experience of being with someone who is more absent than present. As Bion once said, therapy is about helping a patient stop trying to be someone else and start instead to speak from themselves.

When analysis "works" it is because something of this sort does happen: people do recover (or discover) a sense of becoming themselves. This chapter is about some of the ways this process is enabled, and some stories that illustrate that change. "Becoming" is used here in the present continuous because although people often long for the security of a settled identity, none of us ever "become" but are, hopefully, always in the process of becoming. Similarly, "selves" is necessarily plural because as this chapter explores, the self is never singular, and one of the possibilities that therapy offers is the ability to tolerate and even embrace (rather than panic about) the multiplicity and contradictory nature of our many selves.

Working with someone who is talking about, but not *from*, themselves can feel disturbing and disorientating. Someone may verbally express a longing for change whilst communicating a strong but unspoken sense of not wanting to move from the security of the familiar. As examples throughout this book illustrate, clinging to the prescribed and known, however constricting it is, can feel a more attractive proposition than facing a visceral dread of the unknown.

Freedom and safety are often curiously inseparable, and frequently in analysis there is a tension between venturing towards the new then hunkering back down in retreat to the known. The next story explores how both subjective and objective resistances to change can influence this tension between opening up and closing down.

Resisting change

A woman in her early forties has for several months now been swamped by a debilitating sadness and exhausted by insomnia. I have been working with her for several years and these symptoms are fairly recent. She first came to therapy when she and her partner had begun the process of starting a family through donor-sperm conception. My patient was anxious that this would make relations with her own mother even more fraught than they were, as her mother already found her lesbian identity immensely difficult to accept.

Nearly five years later, she is the mother of two healthy children and still in therapy. Her relationship with her partner and children is thriving. She talks about the experience of mothering in a visibly joyful way, and on the occasions when she has brought one of her babies to a session her deep and loving contentment is palpable. But her relationship with her mother continues to be distressingly problematic.

Her mother's unaffectionate ambivalence about both my patient's sexual identity and her children's unknown paternity makes my patient desperate for her approval, and although she is aware that this need routes back to many childhood experiences of never feeling good enough in her mother's eyes (and that this, in turn, is what her own mother experienced from her grandmother) she can't stop herself from trying to elicit a gesture of approval that her brother gets in spades simply by existing.

As she is the one who conceived the children, and as her partner's work is more lucrative and secure, my patient is the main carer. Over the last couple of years she has run herself ragged in her need to prove to the world and to her mother (which, for her, almost amount to the same thing) that although her family may not equate with the norm, her mothering skills are second to none.

Living significantly out of kilter with our fuller needs always triggers a compensatory reaction and this woman's neglected life began to kick back as irritability and exhaustion. Someone who usually took pains over her appearance, she started coming to sessions looking listless and uncared for and often described feeling pervaded by a sapping sadness. "Something in me has become lost," she often said, and insomnia and depression were the words she often used to describe what had taken over.

The insomnia was something she increasingly dreaded. She usually got off to sleep alright but woke with a bolt of panic in the early hours, often startled by a dream. These dreams, she told me, are mostly a variation on the same theme. "I am by my front door and someone is knocking. It is a glass door and I can see that it is a woman with children. I know her from other dreams and am terrified of her anger. In this dream she hammers at my door with ugly fury. In another dream she smashes the glass, enters the house and although I feel petrified I have to go with her. She shows me a room I have never noticed before, a small, dark and dusty study packed with books."

Without the space here to describe anything more than the briefest of her associations, she responded to the dream by focussing on why the study room had become dusty and dark and why the woman (who she identified as herself) had become so destructively angry. She recognised just how damaging her need to prove to her mother that she was good enough had become, and that desperately giving out to others in the perfect mummy way, but not taking enough in for herself, was creating the backlashing anger.

Her associations to the dream study included her talking about how her choice to become a mother had involved closing the door on an MA in fine art. As she talked about this aspect of herself, her liveliness was visibly rekindled and she became energised in a way I had not seen in her for a long while. Soon after exploring this dream she decided to find a way of picking up again where she had left off and reapply to the course.

Yet more than a year passed before this decision took any practical shape. Initially this was because of her own resistance to change: returning to study meant giving up the image she had created of herself as the full time and perfect mother, and she could be as critical of herself as her own mother could be of her. But she overcame this resistance, was accepted on to the course she wanted, and thrived from immersing herself in a world she had always been drawn to. The depression began to lift as she became energized by living from more of herself.

However, her new source of empowering pleasure unsettled some of those around her. A close friend, threatened by her tilt from neediness to strength, was ambivalent rather than supportive. Her children intuited her guilt and used it, when they were tired, to say they didn't want anyone else to collect them from school. Her mother was almost triumphantly attacking about the pitfalls of trying of juggling too many conflictual needs. These backlashes unsteadied my patient and for a while she was a hair's breadth from stopping the course because of the negative impact of these resistances to her change.

Breaking down

Change is always a Janus-headed beast. We both want it and fear it. We encourage yet envy it in others. We need people to stay put or we lose our bearings, yet we need them to depart from the familiar or life becomes stultified. It is an endless see-saw between maintaining and unsettling the status quo, which we need to be aware of if we are not to betray either our own or others' growing selves.

Significant change always involves the chaos of confusion and even if we consciously invite it into our lives it can often feel unmanageable and overwhelming. Often described as a breakdown, the linear safety of a Mondrian canvas is replaced by the uncontained turbulence of Kandinsky. Or, like some of Howard Hodgkin's paintings, the intensity of colour has spilled out of the canvas and on to the no-longer containing frame.

Sometimes a breakdown (especially of a psychotic nature) can be frighteningly dramatic and result in hospitalisation. Mostly, an experience of breaking down stultifying and neurotically restricting ways of living happens in a more manageable way, a gradual chipping away of redundant defences and a trickling, rather than flooding in, of what has been denied or not yet embraced. As the next piece explores, how open or closed we are to the underlying meaning of what is happening, and how possible it is to change the circumstances that precipitated it, will determine whether the disturbing experience can be assimilated as constructive or destructive.

A man in his eighties describes the turmoil and disorientation of a breakdown he suffered when younger. "I lived as if under great inner pressure. Everything in the world seemed difficult and incomprehensible. I was in a constant state of tension. I plunged down into dark depths, and couldn't fend off a feeling of panic."

Anyone who has endured the terror of a breakdown can probably identify with his description. A breakdown may emerge from an ongoing depression or merge with one as it unfolds; it can envelop someone slowly or overwhelm them like a terrifying bolt from nowhere. It may be difficult to pinpoint what triggered it or it might be a reaction to some specific external stress. Whatever the cause, a breakdown is always about psychological imbalance. We become uncomfortably disturbed when something that hasn't been consciously assimilated starts breaking through. For the man above, the intensity of his inner life had become too much at loggerheads with his successful and busy outer world. He was the psychotherapist Jung, and his experiences were written into his autobiography, Memories, Dreams, Reflections.

Although different for everyone, the experience of breakdown can often have some common denominators. Physically, people tend to feel continual bodily tension and often are unable to stop themselves from crying. There is frequently a loss of appetite, the desire to sleep and/or the inability to do so, and difficulty in performing even the most basic everyday functions. "Even going to the corner-shop to buy a paper is a nightmare," explained one young man, "because if I speak to anyone I may burst into tears." Emotionally, there is usually a mood of overwhelming sadness, uncontrollable terror, and panic.

Another common experience during a time of breakdown is a terrifying loss of self-identity and fear of madness. As illustrated through the descriptions at the start of this chapter, the "I" who was at the helm feels lost and with this loss of "I" or ego control, the rest of the self spirals into panic. The woman in the story above expressed it as "something has become lost." Another woman describes it as feeling as if "I don't know who I am any more. I've utterly lost my bearings." It is the anguished cry of King Lear before he stumbles into the storm, his familiar world turned upside down, his identity, power, and certainty broken: "O, let me not be mad, not mad, sweet heaven!"

Whether to a greater or lesser degree, most of us can probably identify moments in our lives when we have lost the sense of who we are or where we are going. It is a theme frequently explored in myths and literature: a dark night, a lost way, a dense wood. The outcome is frequently triumphant and transforming: Dante only reaches Heaven by struggling though Hell and Purgatory; Job similarly has to descend to the depths of his own hell before he can experience recovery.

In psychotherapy there is a similar understanding of the need to break restricting ways of identification down in order to let a fuller self-expression through. In Winnicott's language this involves a breaking down of False Self identifications. In Lacan's (early) thinking this involves recovery of full, rather than empty, speech.

For Jung, this is the process of individuation by which the ego becomes informed by the Self more than the persona.

Recovery or discovery

Some analytic theories focus causally on the need to recover what has become lost, others on the more purposeful need to engage with what needs to be found, and this distinction is one I return to later in this chapter. Whichever ways we talk about it, a breakdown is mostly understood as psyche's bewildering and distressing way of both struggling with, and recovering from, an experience of feeling at loss with ourselves. The "regenerative sea of self loss" is how Milner describes this process, regenerative because often it is through the bewilderment of this time that someone stops struggling to be like someone else and starts struggling instead to become themselves. Like a snake needing to slough off a skin that no longer fits, a breakdown is the body's way of saying "enough, these familiar trappings don't work anymore".

The terror that if things fall apart the centre cannot hold, that (as Lear feared) we will be swamped by the anarchy of our madness, is sometimes tragically what happens. But if the turmoil can be managed and endured, if we can attend to what is clamouring to be heard, we can sometimes discover that "we are lived by forces which cannot be controlled but which can essentially be trusted" (Milner, 1988).

Jung had no capacity to resist the force of his breakdown. He made a conscious decision to not fight what was happening but to try and understand the meaning in the madness. He kept what is now known as his *Red Book*, a record of the six years of overwhelming psychosis which, he discovered, was one of the most importantly creative things he ever experienced.

Of course, for most people a breakdown doesn't end in such creative triumph, and for many the end of one crisis can feel like a temporary respite before the onslaught of another suffering. In his autobiography, Jung talks about how vital the support of his family was during his crisis. He also talks about his professional work as having prevented him from being "driven out of my wits". Many people are not so fortunate in having the anchor of a supportive family or an understanding workplace. For many, a breakdown can mean a lifetime on medication, the loss of work, and/or the loss of a loving relationship.

If the trigger was an uncontrollable external stress (the loss of a deeply significant relationship, bullying, racism, and sexual harassment are common triggers of breakdown) avoidance of repetition can feel impossible. As explored in Chapters Four and Five, emotional distress is often rooted in social inequalities that are beyond the capacity of any one individual to shift. What therapy can offer is an understanding of how being more open than closed to our necessarily complicated selves can significantly shift the likelihood of breakdown occurring or returning.

When patients describe their experience of breakdown they often speak of the physical terror of loneliness, the bleak, visceral desolation at feeling utterly stripped down to a place where no one and nothing can reach or touch them. Somewhere in the middle of nowhere, without attachment to anything that feels secure, between what has been lost and what is not yet found, this part of the process of change is, for most, the time of bleakest and most overwhelming uncertainty and self doubt.

Breaking through

And yet it is often during this time of deepest despair that things imperceptibly start to shift. It is as if when we have accepted that the usual ways of doing things just don't work any more, when we have given up trying to fight against and control what is happening, we can be taken by the surprise of something new being felt. The poet Hopkins, who knew the painful despair of depression and breakdown as well as anyone, described these moments of unexpected fresh hope as being when "blue- bleak embers ... fall, gall themselves, and gash gold-vermillion" (Hopkins, 1978a).

The giving up that is necessarily a part of the breaking down now starts to feel less like mourning and loss of what is needed for survival, more like the leaving behind of what has to be detached from if something purposeful is going to develop. There are many ways of describing what it is that has been blocking psychic growth and every person's experience is unique, but frequently a new capacity to respond to the essential otherness or subjectivity of others emerges from a state of breakdown. It is as if what has broken down are the limitations of a narcissistic way of relating. We so often cling to the security of sameness because of an inability to endure the pain that separateness and awareness of our own mortality engenders.

Certainly the "gold vermillion" that can "gash" from the "blue-bleak embers" of a breakdown is often described through a mood of compassion in which others are experienced as essentially different from oneself, and oneself is experienced with a deeper, fuller subjectivity. You can see this in Blake's version of Job's story when, after feeling "pitched past pitch of grief" (Hopkins, 1978b), he becomes aware for the first time of someone else's needs: those of a beggar nearby, to whom he gives a crust of bread. It's as if he can respond empathically to others because he has become released from the limiting self-absorption of his needy despair. Similarly, it is after Lear has howled out his terrors about losing his mind that he is able to move beyond his assumption that the world revolves around him and recognise that he has "ta'en/Too little care" of the poverty and plight of those around him.

Clinical examples

Below are a couple of examples of a similar process occurring during the course of therapy. Whenever something of this kind of shift occurs, it always makes me feel that whatever doubts I have about aspects of psychoanalytic theory, or frustrations with the damaging superiority-complex the profession seems to suffer from, or concerns about the seemingly inevitable power imbalance within the therapeutic relationship, therapy is, nonetheless, something that I believe in.

> A woman in her early twenties has for many years been what could be described as a party animal and it is worryingly clear that the fire she gets from this behaviour is often more destructive than constructive. Her life revolves around sex, drugs, and a frenetically paced social life that seems to leave no time for an experience of solitude or even sleep. During the early months of therapy she often says she is always lonely but never alone.
>
> As she describes her childhood it isn't difficult to understand this lifestyle as a manic flight from the trauma of losing both her mother and a sibling in a car accident when she was much younger. After experiencing these losses, home never felt like somewhere she could be lovingly recognised for who she was, and the emptiness and hunger created by this lack, and the trauma of the early loss, found a way of being temporarily soothed through an eating disorder and the use of booze, drugs, or another's body, which she often used as protection when she faced the nightly terrors of sleep.

Because of these ways in which she coped with her deep anxiety about re-experiencing the terror of earlier loss, she found it profoundly difficult to experience a healthy sense of where she ended and where the other began. Apart from her hunger to have another's body with her to hold as she struggled to sleep, this inability to tolerate separateness expressed itself through an almost adhesive identification with others: of a friend with anorexia she says, "she is just like me"; of another with family problems, "I know exactly what she is going through". The ability to recognise that others are different from, as well as similar to, her is too frightening as it would force recognition of her own separateness and fear of death.

Yet being with this young woman is often less an experience of emptiness and absence, more one of vital, almost visceral presence. Although full of an emptiness that her body tries in a disassociated way to fill with food, she is also somehow very "in" her body, and although preoccupied by a web of chaotic attachments (which often spill into the session in a traffic jam of bleeping texts) there is nonetheless a sense of her struggling deeply with herself through her identifications with the lives of others.

After some time in therapy it is clear that the destructive nature of her cocaine -fuelled lifestyle is becoming unmanageably dangerous. Terrified that there may soon be no way back, she somehow finds within her the strength to retreat. A close friend of the family offers her a containing and supportive space to be in, and over the next few months this young woman courageously endures both emotional breakdown and physical detoxification, an experience which exposes her to the terrors of solitude that she has spent years trying to escape from.

After several months of living her own dark night of the soul, she emerges with a profound sense of aliveness that she describes as feeling like both recovery and discovery. A new feeling of inhabiting her own body with what she expresses as "earthed joy" communicates itself in the ways she is with others. Like Lear's recognition that he has been too preoccupied with himself to notice the reality of others, she now responds to those closest to her with a new and often overwhelming recognition of their particularities, recalling in sessions the pleasure she felt at hearing a particular voice, gesture, a turn of phrase.

She delights in her new-found capacity to experience herself as being both apart from, as well as a part of, others and reminds me of a child who has just discovered the delight in riding a bicycle and wants to repeat this new bodily experience of trusting some instinctive balance over and again. In the therapeutic relationship there is a similarly new sense of our being alive both separately and together.

During one session she describes the changes she has experienced in an image that becomes pivotal to our subsequent work. "I used to spend all my time needing outside fluff (she gestures with her hands at this point as if brushing away some feathery thistledown), all that frenetic non-stop craziness that meant I never had to be alone. I was never alone. But I was always lonely. And now I am often alone. I can cry, now, and feel pain and some deep sorrow. But I can also feel happy when alone. And I'm far, far less lonely." At this point in the session she turns to me and smiles with "earthed joy" gladness and says: "I wish you could see what I am feeling just now without all that fluff."

The image of William Blake's "Glad Day" unexpectedly comes to mind, a painting that for me embodies vibrancy and joy, and I deliberate about whether or not to share this with her. She has studied art and so it is possible that she knows the piece. I hesitate because her capacity to feel healthily separate in the presence of the other is still quite fragile and I do not want to rekindle her need to feel that there is no gap between where she ends and I begin, that what she feels will automatically be felt by me. And yet the image is so purposefully apposite and her need to have her new experience of feeling real recognised is so strong. So I do tell her what came to mind as she described how she was feeling.

She does not know the picture, and the session ends, but at the start of the next one she mentions the image that she has subsequently found, and in a voice that spoke to me, rather than at me or with me, she smiled and just said "yes".

In a very different way the next example is also about how breaking down some of the ways we unconsciously use to defend ourselves from the pain and vulnerability of aloneness can lead to bewildering chaos, but that out of this both a transforming recognition of others subjectivity and a deeper experience of our own aliveness can emerge.

A man in his late sixties is mortified to find himself in therapy. He has always thought of people who need therapy as needy, weak, and ill and has never seen himself in this light. Literally, as well as emotionally, he finds it difficult to sit comfortably in the patient's chair. He fidgets and picks at bits of fluff from the sleeve of his jacket finding (like the woman above) ways to avoid engaging with the uncomfortable experience of uncertainty.

He has come to therapy because of a make-or-break ultimatum from his wife who has reached the end of her tether about what she describes as his "impossible-to-live-with emotional unavailability". He knows that his behaviour over the years has hurt and frustrated her but has never really understood what she is on about, nor has he felt it necessary to try. Women, he tells me, just do get hysterical like that from time to time and maybe there isn't much that can be done about it. At least that's what he thought until she threatened to leave him. This time he panicked at a recognition that his wife meant what she said. He loves her and very much wants the marriage to work and so has decided to do something that will at least show willing.

At our first session he informs me that he likes to know where he is going with things so has brought along some objectives he hopes to achieve in therapy. For the next couple of months he addresses me without much eye contact and in a way that makes me feel I am a minion at some board meeting and I begin to understand where his wife may be coming from.

For about eighteen months I both hear about, and experience first hand, how his workaholic life style has enabled him to ward off any experience of mutuality, trust, uncertainty, and vulnerability. An archetypal male grump, he had been immersed since the age of seven in an almost totally male world in which big boys do not cry and the choice in relationships is between controlling and being controlled.

Several months into our work together and I was beginning to slightly despair of finding any chink in this intractably defended armour when during one session an opening appeared. One of his colleagues suffered from depression and unexpectedly needed hospitalisation. My patient only reported this event in passing and in a tone of mild irritation because this colleague's absence was going to affect his own work load, and yet this colleague had been a senior partner at his production company for many years.

Unsettled by the depth of his disassociation, I shared my surprise at his response with him. For some reason my words hit home in a way they had never managed to before, and he responded as if his world had suddenly ground to a halt. It is always a mystery to me how we can all resist uncomfortable self-awareness for years on end and then suddenly experience a painful light bulb moment. For whatever reason, having his disregard of someone's emotional pain reflected back at him at that moment opened up floodgates of remorse, self reflection, and significant subsequent change.

For many weeks following this, sessions were full of mortification and shame as he reviewed his life with a different lens. "I have for years treated my wife as a second class citizen without realising it," he told me one day in despair. For several months this new vulnerability made him deeply insecure and clingy, less in the therapeutic relationship, more towards his wife. Separation from her made him very anxious and needy of repeated reassurances of love.

But gradually, his courageous willingness to own his vulnerability rather than project it on to others enabled something new to develop. Therapy became a space where his uncertainties could be painfully experienced. The fidgeting with fluff almost ground to a halt. Eye contact became more comfortable and a profoundly moving sense of this man taking on board what I describe in Chapter One as the "shadow" side became possible. The prescriptive agendas that used to be presented at the beginning of sessions gave way to a new capacity to arrive reflective and empty-headed.

When I commented on this one day he replied contentedly: "Yes, empty-headed and light-hearted". The light-heartedness was playful and delightful and fuelled by the changes that were happening in his marriage. He often described how deeply enriching and loving his relationship with his wife was becoming.

He was also often bewildered by how intensely he now sometimes felt towards the world around him. One day he began a session with a description of something that had happened to him on his way to therapy. Whilst waiting for his train he had felt an overpowering sense of being deeply moved by all the different people milling around, all of them busy with their own lives and journeys. "I just felt an overwhelming compassion for their different joys and pains and a sense of connection with our common humanity."

Both of the people described above courageously experienced their fixed self-identities becoming broken down and challenged and changed. For both of them this change was illustrated in the ways they used their respective worlds. The young woman's use of drugs, sex, and booze to protect her from a painful recognition of her own separateness, and the man's use of work to cut him off from feeling his emotional vulnerability, gave way to encounters with their worlds that felt deeply transformative.

Transformational object use

Bollas has written about the different ways in which we often use our external worlds to facilitate experiences of aliveness and becoming (Bollas, 1987) and the next piece explores how our relationship with both the inanimate and animate in our worlds can be either limitingly narcissistic or purposefully generative.

A woman arrives for therapy looking like a cat with a bowl of cream. After many months of planning she has purchased her very own sports car. She has just turned forty and says that, sitting at the wheel with the roof down, she feels half her age. Listening to her, I am initially reminded of another patient, also a woman, who at about the same age bought a small sailing boat. Like the sports car woman, her purchase was accompanied by a mood of euphoria. Yet there the comparison ends. For in a very fundamental way their purchases stemmed from entirely different impulses and answered significantly different needs.

There is a book by the psychoanalyst Erich Fromm called *To Have or To Be?* in which he distinguishes between the having mode, when we are driven by an acquisitiveness to possess something or someone in our environment to make ourselves feel superficially better, and the being mode, which is about relating to the objects in our world in a way that makes us feel more deeply alive. Fromm's distinction reminds me of Winnicott's ideas about creative object use: how the ways we relate to "things" in our world, human and non-human, either facilitate or restrict emotional growth and aliveness.

For the woman above, buying the sports car was essentially driven by a needy narcissism. Throughout her life she had come to depend upon others' admiration of and desire for her: for the kinds of reasons explored in Chapter Five, she had never internalised a sense of herself as being good enough and learned that, by becoming the object of men's desire. this feeling of lack temporarily vanished. Recently she had become painfully aware that heads didn't turn and gaze in the way they used to, and this had plunged her into a depression. All this, she believed, was, at least for the moment, changed because when seated in her new sports car she felt decades younger and replete with the attention it brought her.

By contrast, the other woman's hunger for a boat was nothing to do with how the world would perceive her. Sailing opened up an aspect of herself that in her busy life had long been dormant. As a child she had been able to, as Winnicott describes it, play alone in the presence of the other, so she did not need the other to provide cover for an inner lack. The boat was loved for its craft and beauty but, even more, for where it could take her emotionally and physically. Whenever she described the pleasure it gave her, her language became less self-centred. She became immersed in the landscape of sea, sky, sun, and wind. She felt free and full of possibility and deeply alive.

Of course most people's everyday use of objects is on a far smaller scale than sports cars and sailing boats, and sometimes it can be difficult to clearly distinguish between the having and being modes: a highly qualified woman, for example, is tempted to do an umpteenth training at great cost in terms of both time and money. She is uncertain whether her desire is propelled by the satisfaction of having even more letters after her name, or by a genuine hunger for, and love of, the subject; or both. A man is in love and fearful of being abandoned, an emotion he has experienced too much of in the past. He has been buying his partner a lot of presents, and wonders if this generosity is partly his way of trying to secure the relationship as well as them being genuine tokens of affection, but the distinction between his genuine delight in his lover and his narcissistic longing to be loved in return feels blurred.

Enduring frustration

The capacity to shift from relating to our worlds in an emotionally needy, potentially split, way to being able (at times at least) to feel open to and changed by the essential otherness of things is, it seems to me, an important benchmark of change in therapy. It connects to Bion's frequent observation that growth becomes possible when we are able to face and endure, rather than split from and avoid, the pain of frustration. Most of the emotional changes described so far in this book have involved people finding, within themselves, the capacity to endure the frustration of emotional uncertainty rather than continue to rely on the reductive security of the prescriptive and habitual.

This question of how able we are to endure frustration is a return to where this book began: as therapists do we face and endure, or split from and avoid, when confronted with the frustration of our own uncertainties? Like the "loss of self" descriptions used at the start of this chapter, most of us have probably experienced the "Who am I as a therapist?" anxiety. Sometimes, like many of the people described throughout this book, we probably retreat to the security of something known. At other times we can hopefully endure not knowing and, like the people described above, experience our therapeutic self as selves, multiplicities of continual potential rather than any rigidly fixed identity.

What will you do with my story?

As I explained in the Introduction, the title of this book—"what will you do with my story?"—was a question asked of me about twenty years ago by one of the first people I worked with as a psychotherapist. She asked this question after describing how she had been sexually abused by both her uncle and father.

I can no longer clearly remember how I responded, either to her specific question or more generally throughout the session, but I do remember feeling anguished and disturbed by what she was telling me and also very conscious of an anxiety that I should be doing something with the distressing story she was telling me about, so feeling the "pressure on the analyst to know all the answers" (Bion, 1978, p. 45). I am sure my responses were inadequate and came from an inability to let something happen in its own time. I am sure I tried to defend myself from the terrible pain of what she was describing by attempting to think about it rather than just be with it.

Probably as a result of this response on my part she never returned, but her question often returns: "what will you do with my story?" Thinking about both her question and the session that it emerged from has made me, over the years, begin to understand that trying to find the right thing to say is invariably a way of defending oneself from the pain of someone else's experience, and that being a therapist is not about being an expert who knows something the patient does not, but is about being able to emotionally engage with the difficult and uncertain process of struggling for change.

Some time after this I was working with a woman who was telling me the details of a dream. It was a dream that involved her climbing down a ladder and as she told me about it I felt quite startled, as her dream imagery matched some lines of poetry that had unexpectedly come into my mind earlier in the session. I had shelved these as belonging to the private, separate part of myself in the work, but now, although I hesitated, I gave in to some impulse to share this experience and tell her the lines from a Yeats poem which had earlier come to mind:

> Now that my ladder's gone
> I must lie down where all the ladders start
> In the foul rag and bone shop of the heart.

> (Yeats, 1933)

This moment was something of a breakthrough in the development of my work as a therapist. I began to increasingly trust my own unconscious processes, and to better understand how moments like these are not separate islands of thought that belong to a hidden part of myself but moods of reverie that both emerge from and feed the energy and mutuality of the therapeutic relationship. The "Glad Day" experience described above is another example of this kind of moment.

Being guided by intuition in this way is not always constructive. For people with an underlying psychosis it can be terrifying to experience someone else "knowing" your thoughts. But being led by the experience of what is happening more than by pre-formulated theory or explanation is, I believe, how therapy can enable significant emotional growth. We all need theories, but if we cannot be vulnerable to losing what we think we need to know whilst engaging with our patients, if we are unable to respond to someone's unique subjectivity because we are blinkered by what we think we should be looking for, therapy will not be a space through which deep emotional change can occur. As O'Connor writes: "Interpretation, specification, delineation, and creation of relationships is the work of psychoanalysis" (O'Connor, 2010, p. 172).

Leaps in the dark

Since the experience of using the lines from a Yeats poem, I have found, and felt affirmed by, writers who naturally integrate this approach into their work as therapists. Jung, Milner, Winnicott, Khan, Bion, Coltart, Meltzer, Bollas, Ogden, and Orbach all emphasise being led by experience rather than leading with explanation. Reik bluntly and reassuringly puts it: "I did not give a damn about logic and what I had learned in the books. I did not think of any psychoanalytic theory. I just said what had spoken in me despite and against all logic and I was correct" (Reik, 1988).

Like those who use a phenomenological approach to inform their work, many of these writers also emphasise how listening with the whole of one's body enables "leap in the dark" moments to occur (Meltzer, 1992,), intersubjective experiences that enable "acts of freedom" (Symington, 1986) from the need to "do" something to or for the patient. Such moments are mutative and mutual (Balint, 1986, Jung, 1957, Symington, 1986) and, because they are essentially about being open to the fecundity of unconscious processes, they remind us that we are all selves in the process of becoming.

As mentioned in different places throughout this book, psychoanalysis often makes a distinction between a regressive or progressive interpretation of material, a differentiation between restoring what has become lost and evolving what has not yet been (e.g., Bion, 1970, Jung, 1921). Awareness of the many different time dimensions in therapeutic work is, as Ellis has explored, an important part of any therapeutic work. Growth often involves letting go of a longing for what is experienced as being lost, and discovering that both tolerance of separation and an awareness of mortality can heighten our feeling of aliveness in the present (Ellis, 2008).

If, as therapists, we can let the present immediacy and specificity of a patient's speech guide our responses, we are more likely to enable potential growth to occur. We are not The Ones Who Know. The story is never something we "do to". The process of engaging with someone's story makes both our patients and ourselves challenged and changed. And importantly, unlike analysis, someone's story never ends. All we can hope for is that therapy can enable someone to live their story beyond therapy with a deeper and more vibrant experience of their own unique and necessarily complex subjectivity.

References and suggested reading

Balint, M. (1986). The unobtrusive analyst. In: G. Kohon (Ed.), *The British School of Psychoanalysis, the Independent Tradition*. London: Free Association Books.

Bion, W. R. (1970). *Attention and Interpretation*. London: Tavistock. (Reprinted London: Karnac 1984).

Bion, W. R. (1978). *Four Conversations with W. R. Bion*. Perthshire: Clunie Press.

Bollas, C. (1987). *The Shadow of the Object: Psychoanalysis of the Unthought Known*. London: Free Association Books.

Carroll, L. (1932). *Through the Looking Glass*. London: Macmillan.

Ellis, M. L. (2008). *Time in Practice, Analytical Perspectives on the Times of Our Lives*. London: Karnac.

Fromm, E. (1978). *To Have or To Be?* London: Jonathan Cape. (Reprinted London: Abacus, 1988).

Hopkins, G. M. (1978a). The Windhover. In: W. H. Gardner (Ed.), *Poems and Prose*. Harmondsworth: Penguin.

Hopkins, G. M. (1978b). The dark sonnets. In: W. H. Gardner (Ed.), *Poems and Prose*. Harmondsworth: Penguin.

Jung, C. G. (1921). Definitions. In: *Psychological Types, C. W. 6* (Trans. H. G. Baynes). London: Routledge, 1977.

Jung, C. G. (1957). Principles of practical psychotherapy. In: *The Practice of Psychotherapy, C. W. 16*. (Trans. H. G. Baynes). London: Routledge, 1993.

Jung, C. G. (1964). *Memories, Dreams, Reflections*. London: Routledge & Kegan Paul.

Meltzer, D. (1992). *The Claustrum*. London: Karnac.

Milner, M. (1988). *The Hands of the Living God*. London: Virago Press.

O'Connor, N. (2010). Listening differently in the face to face. In: *Questioning Identities: Philosophy in Psychoanalytic Practice*. London: Karnac.

Reik, T. (1988). The surprised psychoanalyst. In: B Wolstein (Ed.), *Essential Papers on Countertransference*. New York: University Press.

Symington, N. (1986). The analyst's acts of freedom as agent of therapeutic change. In: G. Kohon (Ed.), *The British School of Psychoanalysis: The Independent Tradition*. London: Free Association Books.

Symington, N. (2002). *A Pattern of Madness*. London: Karnac.

Winnicott, D. W. (1956). Primary maternal preoccupation. In: *The Maturational Process and the Facilitating Environment*. London: Hogarth Press, 1990.

Yeats, W. B. (1933). "The Circus Animals' Desertion". In: *Collected Poems of W. B. Yeats*. London: Macmillan. (Reprinted 1981).

Marion Milner interview for *Everywoman* (published September 1992)

Many people have identified with the words Marion Milner wrote at the beginning of her autobiographical work, *A Life of One's Own*: "It was gradually dawning on me that my life was not as I would like it and that it might be in my power to make it different ... I was drifting without rudder or compass, swept in all directions by influence from custom, tradition, fashion ... Was there no intuitive sense of how one should live, something like the instinct that prompts a dog to eat grass when he feels ill?"

Based on a diary she started when she was twenty-six, the book was first published under the pseudonym Joanna Field in 1934. Recently reprinted, it is as pertinent today as it was nearly sixty years ago. It is a remarkable piece of writing: Virginia-Woolf-like in its stream of consciousness style, poetic in its prose, disarming in its emotional honesty and insight. Marion Milner once called it a kind of detective story in which she, as much as the reader, is surprised by what she finds during her hunt for a "central purpose in life", and certainly it has the compulsive quality which hallmarks that genre.

The method of her search in *A Life of One's Own* is as remarkable as her findings. Discovering that free writing and drawing revealed the neglected, repressed parts of herself, Marion Milner stumbled on her unconscious years before the tools of psychoanalysis had become part of general knowledge. In the long term, the diary that she started at the age of twenty-six proved to be a kind of lodestar. Astonished by what her discovery of unconscious processes revealed, Marion Milner eventually trained as a psychoanalyst. Although her background is Freudian-cum-Kleinian, her theories have shifted to accommodate new experiences, and today she is deeply influenced by the more mother–child centred work of Winnicott. She also continued to paint and write. All her work carries the same hallmark, the stamp of what she learned from writing *A Life of One's Own*; namely that her own lived experience rather than others' frames of reference must be the touchstone for truth.

Marion Milner will be ninety-two this year, and in the sixty years that have passed since she wrote *A Life of One's Own* both her own world and the world around her have undergone profound changes. Many of her ideas are now so much part of analytical and feminist language that it is easy to forget, when reading her books, that she was very much a pioneer in uncharted territory. One thing that hasn't changed is her home. Ever since the birth of her son, in 1932, she has lived in the same house at Chalk Farm.

Taller and more statuesque that I had imagined, Marion Milner's face, her eyes, her whole being exude the warmth and openness that is so present in her books. Sitting on the analytical couch in her back room, I find myself talking far more than I normally would in an interview. I am, I remind myself, in the presence of a professional listener, someone who is well used to redirecting questions. I am also in the room of someone whose interest in life is not only undiminished, but also vibrant. She gestures to the book she is reading at present, mentions a television programme she has recently seen, tells me she is going to the Rembrandt exhibition that week, and asks if I have been. She also makes clay figures and draws from them, meditates "a bit", and regularly attends seminars on the ideas of Winnicott. With a mind so active, does she miss her psychoanalytic work, her patients? "Yes, I do. I stopped seeing patients eighteen months ago as my memory was getting bad. I feel sad at how much better I could have done if I knew then what I know now."

This willingness to continually remould her ideas in the light of new experience is very present in her writing. So how much have the thoughts and theories she explored in her earlier books changed? What about her ideas on bisexuality for example? First explored in *A Life of*

One's Own, the notion that within each of us there is an inherent conflict between masculine and feminine ways of being is perhaps the cornerstone of all her writing. "I still don't know what people mean by 'masculine' and 'feminine'. I'm looking at a book by a Jungian called Singer on Blake: *The Unholy Bible*. Singer calls the ability to have relationship female, whereas Winnicott in his paper *To Be or Not To Be* thinks female is being, male is doing or *being done to*. Most people see *being done to* as a female characteristic. I'm still unsure. I'm still studying what people mean by male and female. I think we use them too loosely."

"Being done to" is something she has written much about. In her second book, *Experiment in Leisure*, which she also refers to as "a study in the use of masochism", she reflects on the tendency of many women (including herself) to be self sacrificing and unassertive. Why do so many women find it so difficult to live for themselves rather than through the needs of others? "Like all these nature/nurture things it's difficult to know how much is inborn. Do women have a more introverted nature, or do what's expected of them?"

This conflict between self assertion and submission to another's needs is particularly evident when she writes about motherhood. Wanting children, Marion Milner also feared the sacrifice of freedom this might involve. "Perhaps it is more of a practical than psychological conflict now than it was for me. I went back to work after the birth of my son. It wasn't a great battle over choice. It was necessity. My husband was ill. Do I think it makes any difference for the child? I think it depends on what the mother's like when she's there. I wouldn't have been very good at it!"

It is this characteristic reluctance to generalise from the particular that shines through in her writing. The integrity of the individual always matters more than theory or tradition. This is clearly reflected in her approach to Christianity. As a child she went to a Church of England boarding school, but later stopped going to church services as she felt they killed the spirit of the thing they professed. Yet her writing and painting are rich in biblical quotations and religious images. "For me the main thing is what Blake said: "All religions are different manifestations of each nation's poetic genius." What goes wrong is when the various religions insist that they alone have the absolute and literal truth."

What of the dilemma faced by the growing number of people who are uncomfortable with organised religion but still feel a need for ritual at times of stress and important change? It is an issue that crops us regularly in her writing. In her most recent book, *The Suppressed Madness of Sane Men*, Marion Milner describes how a patient of hers, a boy of eleven, enacted sacrificial rituals during play as a way of integrating previously denied parts of himself. As we discuss this psychological need for ritual, Marion Milner talks of the plans she has made for her own funeral. I wonder if she is afraid of death, of dying. "No, oh no! What frightens me is the idea I might live too long. My doctor said: 'If you go on taking the angina pills you'll probably live to be a hundred and five.' God forbid! I want to die here, you see. I don't want to go into hospital, or an old people's home."

She offers to show me some of her paintings, and as we make our way upstairs I understand why she fears leaving her home. It is a beautiful house, rambling and rich with pictures and photographs from past and present. A wooden school from her son's childhood is used as a window prop, while outside, beyond the window, red tulips glow in a lush garden. Their redness seems fitting for someone whose books are so full of a passion for life and the importance of being aware of feelings.

Upstairs, paintings are stacked haphazardly. She shows me some of the originals from *On Not Being Able to Paint*, the book in which she develops her discovery that painting can open doors into the unconscious. She also shows me collages made from torn-off bits of her own "failed" paintings. "They are not planned at all, just playing with colours and shapes. Only when finished do they tell me what they are about. Then they become a kind of inner analyst."

On the wall above us is a pretty harbour scene of Itchenor, near Chichester. "I painted that in 1919 and, for me, it's full of the peace and freedom of the war being just over. My brother was safely back from the navy and my sister from her war work, so she and I went off on bicycles, right across Sussex and down to the sea where we hired a little boat." Dusting down a photograph, she shows me a picture of her brother. I wonder if her family have been at all shocked by her books. Is that why she used a pseudonym? "No, it wasn't because of family reasons. My older cousin once said: 'You know, I don't think your family have any idea what you're talking about!' As for the pseudonym, I used that because I was worried that the free associations in *A Life of One's Own* might frighten the staff at the schools where I was about to start working [as an educational psychologist]."

As we turn to go, she tells me that her sister (Winifred Burger, whose portrait is on the cover of Virginia Woolf's *To the Lighthouse*) died from cancer in the room we were in. The sadness of this image jars painfully with the sweetness of the earlier impression of her cycling young and carefree across Sussex. But then maybe that is an apt way to have ended a meeting with Marion Milner; experiencing what she has spent her life writing about: the difficulty but importance of opposites.

INDEX

aliveness 2
Anon 14–16

Balint, M. 14, 56, 126
Benjamin, J. 12, 68, 89
Bion, W. R. 26, 124, 126
    dangers of formulated knowing
        14
    leaving theory out of practice
        19, 58
    multiple vertices 25–26
    pressure to be the one who
        knows 14
    reverie and intuition, importance
        of 25–26
    toleration of frustration and
        uncertainty, importance of 26,
        124
    unconscious as purposeful 25–26,
        42

without memory or desire 13, 19,
    42, 58
Blake, W.
    Book of Job 2–3
    Glad Day 119
    illustrations: plates 1 and 21,
        4–5
    "The Clod and the Pebble", 74
Bluebeard 94
body, the
    aliveness 36–37, 106, 118
    body hatred 104
    body neglect 104–105
    case histories: fear embedded
        in body: phobia 82–84
    disassociation 37–38, 104, 106,
        118
    earthed joy 118–119
    listening with the body as
        therapist 126

135